Tiger! Tiger! Burning Bright

The Shivnarine Chanderpaul Story

Clifford Narinesingh

ROYARDS PUBLISHING COMPANY
7A Macoya Industrial Estate, Macoya Trinidad W.I.
Telephone: 868-645-0423, 663-6002
Fax: 868-663-3616
E-mail: royards@aol.com
Website: www.royards.com
e-book format – digitalcanopi.com

Clifford Narinesingh

ISBN: 978-976-8303-84-4(Paperback)

Tiger! Tiger! Burning Bright
The Shiv Chanderpaul Story
(Authorized)

First Published: February 2022

Published by: Royards Publishing Company

Layout and graphic design: Dwight Narinesingh
Typeset: Diamond Coutain-Rambaransingh
Printed by:

Major works by the author:
The Growing with Language Series
The Comprehensive English Series
Developing Language Series
Language Around Us Series
Creative English Series
Insights
Sunshine and Shadow
English for Special Purposes
Like Leaves to a Tree (ed)
(album of family poems)
Gavaskar: Portrait of a Hero
The Presence of Tendulkar
Lara: The Untamed Spirit
Mr. Solo-
The Legendary Ken Charles

Author
Clifford Narinesingh

Table of Contents

For
Leighton Reid
and
Jonah Clifford
Masters of their own turf.

FOREWORD

Shivnarine Chanderpaul earned himself a prominent place in the annals of West Indian Cricket history. In a long and praiseworthy career Shiv established numerous individual records and will continue to be an inspiration to many aspiring cricketers.

The history of West Indies Cricket is embellished by the exploits of countless pioneers – not merely based on ability to bat and/or bowl, but for their flair and panache. Exotic stroke-play, flashing shots, exuberance and enthusiasm, flamboyant characters, all became common hallmarks of the allure of West Indies Cricket.

As the game itself developed, the West Indian has always been an influential catalyst – bringing a unique "something" which enhanced it and added to its popular appeal. It is this sense of "unique" which defines Chanderpaul – from his humble beginnings to his longevity, from his unorthodox stance to his insatiable appetite for accumulating runs: all encapsulated in an unassuming approach to his game in which he seemed to be striving to master the functional as opposed to putting on the style.

Shiv tells his own story in much the same as he developed his own unique batsmanship. His was a relentless pursuit of success: practice, practice and more practice; concentration on getting the basic fundamentals right and minimizing any mistakes in his game. These are the traits which he displayed consistently throughout a career in which he was respected and admired by team-mates and opponents as well as by fans across the international spectrum.

As a youngster falling in love with the game, Chanderpaul would have been conscious of the great Guyanese heroes of previous times – Rohan Kanhai, Basil Butcher and Joe Solomon; and of more recent vintage, Alvin Kallicharan, Roy Fredericks and Clive Lloyd – but while he never sought to copy them, he certainly wanted to emulate (or even surpass) them.

It would also be erroneous to simply see Chanderpaul as a quiet introvert, or his batting as cautious. In his own way he played each innings as he determined --- as a long rearguard action or some among the fastest Test centuries. Who could forget that ODI vs Sri Lanka at the Queen's Park Oval when, with 9 wickets down and facing the last over bowled by Chaminda Vas, he hit the final two balls for a 4 and a 6 to snatch victory for the West Indian uncharacteristic? Shiv carved out his own method, developed his own characteristics and joined his illustrious compatriots at the top of West Indies' batting firmament.

Shiv's individual success is all the more remarkable when placed in the context of the turmoil of West Indies Cricket, during much of his time in the team. There was increasing disharmony between West Indies players and administrators and West Indies Cricket was losing its hard-earned lustre. Even at the beginning of his career, it was obvious that the team was not performing as a No.1 ranking implied, yet it took defeat by Australia in 1995 to be "officially" recognized. Almost immediately thereafter, West Indies Cricket was in free fall reaching a No.8 ranking.

This must have been a particularly difficult time for that generation of West Indies players to suddenly find themselves being vilified rather than enjoy the unabashed hero-worship heaped on so many of their predecessors.

Obviously "the fall" did not just happen in 1995. There was a gradual melt down over a number of prior years – a decline, however, being ignored by successive administrations that would also have impacted team dynamics and relationships as well as individual players and their development. Through it all, Chanderpaul – and others like Lara, Curtley Ambrose and Courtney Walsh – shone through. How was that possible?

Chanderpaul's perspective shared in the following pages may not provide answers but it certainly provides important information. Information and lessons which will be useful to all those who have responsibility for charting the way forward for West Indies Cricket. The descent from a number one ranking into the lower echelons was a virtual "free-fall". The journey back to the top will be long and arduous – so it is important to go "back to the basics" armed with the experience of the immediate past.

In the overall context of the state of West Indies cricket during his career, all the more kudos to Chanderpaul – well done Shiv and thank you.

Deryck Murray

Former West Indian Test cricketer – (wicket keeper/batsman)

PREFACE

The latter part of the 90s to the present time has not been a period of delight in West Indian cricket. The glory of former years faded to one of dejection and disillusionment. Who would have thought that the fall would have been so sudden and then follow so long? Our cricket literature bulges with accounts of brilliant careers of players who have excelled and distinguished themselves on the world's playing fields. Some have performed with excellence by virtue of their natural talent or through some indefinable divine gift and others have worked relentlessly to construct solid careers. Many of them have impacted the lives of the younger generation and transformed the lives of many.

In the cricketing world, we have read about or witnessed the incredible feats or exploits of daring achievements which not only announce man's capabilities, but are expressive of the human condition's ability to face the sporting challenges that life offers.

If we delve into the careers of many of our West Indian cricketers, we will see a pattern which has emerged in terms of their origins and their cricketing progress. The stories of West Indian cricketers from country to country in the 60s and earlier, save for a very few, reveal similar backgrounds – players whose origins were rooted in simple environments. They grew up without the trappings of the more privileged but performed and excelled through their passion, ability, discipline and application. As young initiates, they took delight in playing the games not thinking that accolades lay ahead. In this mold of players who rose to eminence, the figure of Shiv Chanderpaul is impressive. Through his love, passion, intense devotion and resilience he has come to the fore, a gallant player as demonstrated in his commitment and achievements.

This narrative relates the cricketing life of Shiv from his formidable debut against England in the year 1994 to his premature retirement in 2015, after 21 years of salvaging pride for the former universe bosses in cricket. It relates in some significant detail, the course of his life growing up in a small rural village called Unity outside of Georgetown, Guyana. The account here makes no claim to any deep sociological analysis of West Indian cricket. It simply traces his development and contribution in the path of West Indian cricket during its continuing decline from the mid-90s.

Cricketing details of matches are highlighted relating Shiv's presence and performance amidst West Indies decline. Some readers may not be in tune with details but they are significant if we are to asses his contribution to the game. The minute details of some matches are designed to emphasize his role in the middle order as his resilience and courage were a lesson for his teammates.

What emerges is the ascendancy of an individual whose skill, application, discipline and deep desire to achieve for his self-esteem, team, country and region. Such a career deserves recognition and serves as a model for generations of youth to consider, not only in sport but their various paths in life. The overriding theme details the cricketing performance of one whose challenge was to save his team from the abyss into which it was falling.

The West Indies' decline from 1995 to the present has been

rapid with only short flattering periods of seeming resurgence. It may be described as a fall from grace, a sense of inertia, loss of soul and lack of discipline and motivation. We have moved from the glorious days of success and invincibility into an area of darkness.

Over the years, the crises have become more complex with continuous impasse and feuding between players and the West Indies Cricket Board. Such crises have led rival teams to benefit from the divisiveness and lack of cohesiveness in Caribbean cricket. The forces of mighty opposites (Board and Players) have disturbed the path to positive and delightful cricket.

It ought to be mentioned at this point, and it is demonstrated throughout the book that Shiv stood up while the others around him were falling. Isn't it a paradox that Shiv's rise took place in the midst of a failure of the players and repeated conflict between players and the West Indian Cricket Board of Control? During this period of decline which was evident since 1995, Shiv carried the team in the way George Headley (Atlas) carried the team in the 1930s.

Here is how CLR James describes Headley's Olympian performances for the West Indies in a time where there was little support around him.

Between 1930 and 1938 Bradman had with him in England Ponsford, Woodfull, McCabe, Kippax, Brown, Hassett. All scored heavily. In 1933 and 1939 West Indian batsmen scored runs at various times, but George had nobody who could be depended on. In 1933 his average in the Tests was 55.40. Among those who played regularly the next average was 23.83. In 1939 his average in the Tests was 66.80. The next batsman averaged 57.66, but of his total of 173 he made 137 in one innings. Next was 27.5. It can be argued that this stiffened his resistance. I don't think so. And George most certainly does not. "I would be putting on my pads and sometimes before I was finished I would hear that the first wicket had gone". This is what he carried on his shoulders for nearly ten years. None, not a single one of the great batsmen, has ever been so burdened for so long.

It is hoped that the blemishes over the years will fade and once greater commitment is demonstrated by all participants, West Indies cricket will achieve a more elevated status among the cricketing nations. The emergence of players with passion, loyalty to team and region, national fervour, self-discipline and self-motivation will certainly make the game once more a delightful experience, and give sustenance and meaning to the West Indian masses.

Clifford Narinesingh

Chapter 1

First Encounters: A Defining Debut

He walked a field modest, and small, and seldom failed to raise our score and spirits.

Edmund Blunden

As dawn broke on the second day of the second Test match between West Indies and England at Bourda Cricket Ground, Guyana, in 1994, the sky came to life as if in sympathy with the human events that were to unfold. Guyana's pride was evident among an elated and enthused crowd celebrating their local hero's selection to the West Indies cricket team. They streamed across the country to hail their hero and offer songs of praise for his ascendancy. They came from the interior, from coastal villages and from distant Berbice to see their hero play beside the already legendary Brian Lara.

A place in a Test team is a most coveted prize. It signifies a recognition of a higher level of performance and of a talent to be nurtured and developed. This was all the more to be welcomed because in the West Indies' performances in recent years, standards have fallen and mediocrity has been very evident at Test level. Our failing now contrasts with the development and improvement of cricket in India, Sri Lanka, New Zealand and Bangladesh where serious efforts are being made to improve and preserve standards.

When England toured the West Indies in 1994, they were

expected to dominate against a team about which, at best, it could be said, was a team in transition. The course of the tour proved to be dramatic and most rewarding, particularly for the West Indies community of cricketers and supporters in the islands.

The tour started off with a West Indian victory at Sabina Park, Jamaica, which inspired greater confidence within the team. Here the score card read – England: 234 and 267; West Indies: 207 and 95/2. Lara's contribution was 83 and Jimmy Adams 95 not out. Keith Arthurton made 126 and then slumped into mediocrity. A West Indian victory in this Test brought a great sense of optimism and hope for a prosperous series.

However, in the second Test at Bourda in Guyana, a decision to omit the Trinidadian, Phil Simmons, from the team and introduce the fledgling Shivnarine Chanderpaul, a Guyanese national, caused some measure of contention; it certainly caused discontent among fellow Trinidadians who felt that the West Indies Board was bowing to Guyana's wishes at their home ground. Once more, the scourge of insularity surfaced as evident from time to time. Some wondered whether the scourge of insularity was about to return in full to West Indies cricket.

Shiv's came into the side mainly as a batsman but was also respected as a bowler. At the age of 19 he was called to the highest form of cricket. It was perhaps a good thing that his first encounter was in the comfort of his home ground. The 'familiar' would have been of great consolation for an initiate.

Many cricketers have disclosed their fear, anxiety and apprehension at the thought of such an occasion. It was a formidable challenge to assert his presence as a batsman in a team that included Brain Lara and Desmond Haynes.

Shiv's debut appearance in this 1994 series was remarkable and memorable. It was not just a brilliant debut but he was witness to events which inspired him for the rest of his life. Here he was in the midst of Lara's ascendancy as he partnered Lara to the historic feat of surpassing Gary Sobers'` record of the highest individual score in the history of Test cricket; he was in the presence of established players such as Desmond Haynes, Richie Richardson, Courtney Walsh and Curtly Ambrose and was part of the team in which Curtly Ambrose devastated the English batsmen for a mere 46, their lowest Test score. It was a defining debut which gave him lessons and inspiration to progress.

Shiv's contribution grew as the series progressed. A remarkable stream of successes marked his entry on the international scene. The scores in the first four Tests were:

Test 1	**Eng**	**234**	**W.I**	**407**	**W.I won**
		267		**95/2**	
Test 2	**Eng**	**322**	**W.I**	**556**	**W.I won**
		190			
Test 3	**W.I**	**252**	**Eng**	**328**	**W.I won**
		269		**46**	
Test 4	**Eng**	**355**	**W.I**	**304**	**Eng won**
		394/7		**237**	

Test 5	**W.I**	**593/5**	**Eng**	**593**	**Match drawn**
		43/0			

Shiv averaged 57.60

He achieved an aggregate of 288 in four Tests and at average of 57.60. His half centuries in each Test were greeted with the praise he deserved. He demonstrated skill and ability to counter first class pace with consummate ease. It was indicative of a growing, burgeoning talent and this meant further bolstering of the West Indian presence. The series was a memorable occasion for Shiv, team, country and the region.

In Shiv's first encounter during the second Test, at Bourda, Guyana, he had been placed in a team which included the proven prowess of players such as Desmond Haynes, Richie Richardson, and Brian Lara and this obviously was a challenge thrown at him – that of adding supremacy to the team. Here he demonstrated an equable temperament as he negotiated the opposing team's armoury. Against the bowlers' arsenal his defence was strong, his strokes well-timed and cleverly executed. Wisden describes his innings as one of 'wristy elegance'. His half century was applauded by an elated crowd, proud and excited as they danced in support of their local hero. The crowd had their hunger for good cricket satisfied with Lara's majesty at the wicket coupled with Adams' masterful display. In addition, Shiv's well-executed innings stirred a sonorous roar from the excited crowd. This debutante showed great physical courage against the pace of Fraser, Salisbury, Lewis and Igglesden.

In response to England's fairly respectable 322, West Indies exemplified superiority through Lara's majestic and imposing 176 and Adams' solid 137. Wisden reports "The ovation on Lara's exit grew to a crescendo at the sight of Chanderpaul" in No. 6 position as he made his entry. This first encounter yielded 62, a promising start for a fledging batsman.

Shiv recalls that the achievement of 62 was a great boost to his self-confidence. For him Bourda was his home ground as he had played many matches there. He felt confident. Shiv was happy "as the crowd gave me full support. It made me more determined to perform.

I had to prove my ability to my teammates who supported me. There were some greats in the team so I decided to be disciplined and alert at the crease and it paid off," Shiv recalls.

In this Test, England suffered a disastrous blow as the West Indies got past the post by an inning and 44 runs. West Indies achieved a total of 556 and this was demoralizing for the English batting. This defeat left the English broken and dispirited. It led Scyld Berry to comment that "like all other English teams it possessed all the resilience and durability of a mayfly".

The third Test at the Queens's Park Oval in Trinidad concluded with great suspense and high drama. In this Test, England held the advantage for three days and were set for victory, going at a target of 194. It was a contest that swung dramatically through a breath-taking spell in the last innings by West Indies pacer, Ambrose, who decimated the English team and reduced it to its lowest innings total of 46. Ambrose's spell was lethal.

Stephen Thorpe of Wisden Cricket Monthly reports: "a denouement both electrifying and shocking in its finality, against one of the most sensational fast-bowling feats of modern times by Curtly Ambrose, will forever remain etched in the annals of Queen's Park Oval and West Indian Cricket".

Amidst all the excitement and dramatic turn of the event, Shiv stood in awe and amazement. A new comer to the team was resolute as he contributed 19 in the first innings and went on to another half century in the second innings when he top-scored with a score of 50. Once more, he had demonstrated his competence against the English attack.

After the departure of the top 5 batsmen, he had rallied to 50 before a hook shot ended his stay at the crease.

Surprisingly to many, a wounded England stood resolute and showed character after their dramatic defeat at Port of Spain. In the Fourth Test at Kensington Oval, Barbados, England emerged victorious through two good batting performances and a determined bowling attack. Set to counter 446 in one day and 22 overs, West Indies collapsed after a determined effort from Lara and Arthurton whose departure saw the innings fall flat.

Shiv's role in the first innings was significant as he had saved the prospect of a follow-on with his top-score of 77. In doing so, he salvaged some respectability for his team. At 134 for 7 and facing the seeming inevitability of a follow-on, Shiv partnered Ambrose and Kenny Benjamin to rescue his team. He had come to the rescue at this juncture in the match with a grand effort. His performances in these three Tests were indicative of his future years, years which would be expressive of his fortitude, courage and determination. In three Tests, he had scored three half-centuries and had batted for almost 16 hours. In this innings, he mixed caution and positive batsmanship successfully as he did throughout his career.

The last Test of this series was remarkable, unique and memorable. Shiv was witness to and played a significant part in the last Test of this series which still lingers in the West Indian's public memory. It was Lara's match. Here in Antigua, he dominated and pulverized England's attack relentlessly as he went past Sir Gary Sobers 365 – a record for the highest individual score that had stood at the top for 36 years.

It was a Test not only of Lara's batting but also his fortitude and strength of will. The expectations of the crowd exerted pressure on his spiritual and emotional frame of mind. It was at this time, that his partner at the other end not only aided but gave mental and emotional support as Lara pursued the record.

Shiv remarked: "During the last Test in Antigua, it was a touch and go event as Brian was tiring after his 300. He seemed to be losing his focus. He was telling me it was hard to go further.

I tried to comfort him – told him to relax and he would reach the record. Just keep fighting. You have reached so far already. You have a little further to go. I remember when he achieved the world record, people were scampering to the ground. Brian was hugging me. It was very special: I will always remember that milestone. I was happy to be part of it."

In Lara's book Beating the Field, he recalls how "Chanderpaul was constantly speaking to me, urging me to keep my concentration and not give it away. For a 19-year-old, he showed an amazing maturity and I shall always be grateful to him for the part he played in my success."

In the process, Shiv, once again more enterprising, registered his 4th consecutive Test half century in an innings of 75 not out. Lara has never forgotten this young lad's effort and support during his ascent. Steadfast, with great courage and cricketing skill, Shiv exemplified the virtues of perseverance and concentration and devotion to the task at hand. His disposition and temperament led him to the success he eventually became.

During Lara's epic performance, the biggest stand of 219 with Shiv was also the longest. There were four rain interruptions during this partnership. Because of weariness, "Lara needed shepherding through the final stages by the impressively mature Chanderpaul," Wisden reports.

Shiv had entered a new realm – intense exposure to the harsh realities of Test cricket. His first series record was expressive of a burgeoning talent, of one who thrust his presence into a cricketing world versus a traditionally well-recognised team. In the process, he did lay a foundation for quick recognition. He also had the unique opportunity of partnering successfully with Brian Lara's monumental and memorable record-breaking feat. Not only did he partner Lara but he also demonstrated to the world his strength of character.

As a tribute to Lara's phenomenal achievement, celebrations – particularly in Trinidad – were excessive with the main public event being a motorcade through the town in honour of Lara. It was Lara, the main actor, accompanied by the supporting actor, Shiv Chanderpaul, in fanfare as they drove to the delight of excited well-wishers.

Though Shiv was only a fledging, West Indian critics exclaimed: What more could be asked of this diminutive hero? How he charmed the crowd with his skill, composure and maturity during that audacious partnership!

This series was an opening episode of promise and excitement for Shiv, a young initiate who was carving an image at the international level. It was a magnificent experience – an exposure to the rewards of successful phenomenal feats. The spirit of euphoria spread across the Caribbean and in the later years, Shiv's success inspired great harmony among a people who respected and loved him for his sense of purpose and his humility in the face of success. Not only in the Caribbean but throughout the cricketing world, he has gained the respect of both mates and rivals.

The hope was that his burst of consistency would continue to flourish. Many were emotionally charged and envisaged "a new kid on the block", a hero whose destiny would be proven with the strong support of his team and administration.

Shiv was selected not only for his batting potential but also for his experience as a leg-break bowler. He was quite effective in domestic matches and also inter-island ones. Of greater claim at that time was his effectiveness vs Pakistan's experienced batsmen in a Guyana match.

In addition to his successful entry into the 1994 series vs England, he was given the opportunities to deliver his leg-breaks in all his four Tests in that series. The following reveals his statistical bowling figures in the series:

Second Test	**16-2-49-0**
Third Test	**5-3-13-0**
Fourth test	**10-4-23-0**
	10-3-30-0
Fifth Test	**21-1-94-1**

In India, in his first Test figures, he registered 20-4-63-1. Though he did not earn wickets, his bowling was economical.

Against New Zealand, apart from his 69 and 61 not out when he topped the batting average, his bowling figures were 3-1-10-0, 2-2-0-0. In the other tours during his career, his batting was more dominant and the use of pace and specialist spin bowling were utilized. As a result he was hardly used and if so, as a relief bowler for the pacemen.

As Shiv continued, his life-time achievements recall the mightiest of deeds performed by his compatriots – Fredericks, Kanhai, Butcher, Kallicharran, Solomon, Lloyd, Gibbs, Bacchus, Hooper and Croft – all former Guyanese players who are among or who contributed to the bloom of Guyanese and West Indies cricket.

It was a long gap, a long blank after the departure of Lloyd in 1985 to the arrival of Shiv in 1994. It is also significant that these former players emerged from an environment that did not cater to the luxuries of many modern-day players. Their story reveals that their success grew out of their own, personal creative skills without the trappings of administrative assistance, cricket academies and other support systems of most modern-day players. A perusal of their records will reveal their significant role in shaping a body of cricketing performance unmatched by major cricketing teams. Shiv, at the outset, was proving that he belonged to that group of memorable players; individuals who emerged not from the village green, or pristine pastures but from a simple, rustic environment and who shaped their destinies through their creative skills.

History has revealed that Shiv's career was propelled by his determination, application and skill, a seriousness of purpose and keenness of discipline – all ingredients for success in any venture. As Shiv continued to grow, the varying forces of success and failure were the challenges he faced. For him there were periods of agony but in the larger equation he emerged a successful, well-developed batsman whose name is well-established, recognized and worthy of emulation. He has been made integral in the literature of the game, a recognition he richly deserves.

Chapter 2

The Early Years

Of the rustic, not the village green

Born August 16th, 1974 in the village of Unity to father Kemraj Chanderpaul and mother Uma Chanderpaul, Shiv Chanderpaul grew up with his sisters, Devi and Geeta, in a rural, rustic environment – a coastal village away from the more bustling and moving towns. It was a setting rural to the core, almost lonely, so tranquil even now that it induces meditation.

In the seventies, Unity was unexplored and almost deserted save for its fishing and farming activities. As you traversed the area, wide expanses of open land populated by white egret lent colour which added variety to the abundant vegetation. It still does. Within such a community the dominant activity each year, accompanying religious or national festivals, was the sporting activity of cricket. Interest was inspired by the West Indian team's dominance at that time. The game was nourished and nurtured by a wider population who embraced the West Indian cricket presence. With great fervour and passion, Shiv's father, Kemraj and his uncle Moonilal, were keen participants at club level. His uncle might have ascended to great heights but for an unfortunate mishap.

As Shiv grew up, he learnt of the exploits of his fellow countrymen who were exemplars. As early as 6-7 years of age he was in active pursuit of the game, trying to master the skills of batting and bowling. This intense desire was fueled by his father who discerned his talent at such tender age. At school, he became the passionate cricketer who left school at times to play in areas near the school, knowing full well his sympathetic sister would secure his books at school.

His learning process began at an early age. Shiv recalls, "In our village practice, my dad and everyone around would bowl at me for hours. It taught me to be tough. I was determined to face anything thrown at me. The bouncers from the big boys in the street toughened me. Sometimes they would soak the ball and pelt me and I had to defend myself with my bat. At home I would apply warm water to the bruises on my skin to ease the pain. But this did not stop me. My father and uncle were there to encourage me.

It was my courage and determination which helped me to continue. The pitch we played on was shorter than Test match pitches so I was at the mercy of fast bowlers. This helped me to handle the best bowlers in Test cricket – Brett Lee, Glen McGrath, Wasim Khan, Waqar Younis. Chaminda Vaas among others."

Shiv recalls the magnanimous support he got from his village friends who were all too ready to bowl at him for hours. They had seen in him the making of a good batsman. He always remembers Ishwar Persad and the Chickoree brothers, Krishna, Darsan and Kunderlall, who would tirelessly bowl to him on the pitch at the playing field. At this time, he developed the passion for long periods at the wicket. It was the same determination that was to bolster the West Indian side when everything seemed lost.

At the age of 10, Shiv was taken to the Everest Cricket Club for cricket trials but was not selected. But it was here that here that Mr. Derrick Atwell saw him at practice and encouraged Shiv's father to take him to the Demerara Cricket Club. Between 10-14 years he played for Demerara club under 16 team. His introduction to the Demerara Cricket Club meant neglect of school as the demands of practice were exhaustive. Shiv eventually left because he could not get home early and the financial burden of travel was another problem. During this period (age 13 ½ years) he had not much choice but to leave school, concentrate on his cricket and help his family as he worked on the fishing boat.

At times he would walk all the way for miles with his determined Uncle Moonilal accompanying him. He was never discouraged, always focusing on countering these challenges. Many times, only a sandwich was given to sustain him at the grounds. Shiv recalls, "I would walk with my uncle for miles, hungry and tired. But I thought about playing for my country as I stuck it out, never becoming frustrated."

It was this determination which was evident in his approach to the sport during his cricketing years.

After leaving school at 13 plus, his days were spent either at cricket practice or working with his dad during his fishing trips. Shiv remarks: "I would wake up in the morning and would prepare to go out to sea. What made it difficult was that it was a sailboat. We had to man the sails, hoist them up, work the rudders and at times I would bail water out from a flooded boat. Some of this I would do, almost naked because I had to preserve my clothes when we were further out at sea and casting the nets. Once the net was cast, I would relax and put my clothes on. This was very difficult for me, mentally and physically. As I got older I had to man the sails and my hands were then unusually hardened as I had to pull the ropes. This prepared me for the difficult catches I would take during cricket matches. My teammates would be surprised to know my hands never hurt on those occasions."

At 13, Shiv joined the East Coast Police Team (2nd Division). Sergeant Gibbon of the Cove and John Police Station was generous to him by transporting him on his motorbike from Unity to the playground. At the age of 14, he played for East Coast Police vs Top Enmore Community Club and was seen by Sheik Mohammed who promptly advised his uncle to get him to the Georgetown Cricket Club so he could play First Division cricket. There, the captain of the club, Gary Nacimento observed him and promised to find him a place but it was difficult as the Club had very experienced and good players. Nacimento saw him as a good prospect for the future.

In an under-16 match, Mark Ferreira of the club, promised him his bat if he had scored 100 and he did succeed with an innings of fluent strokeplay which impressed the club. It was a sporting gesture by Mark and others who saw Shiv at play.

Shiv's sense of gratitude is remarkable. He has never "scorned the base degree by which he did ascend", always expressing appreciation for all who helped him on his way to a successful career.

Those early years saw Shiv move from Under 16-19, and

play his way through 2nd and 3rd Division cricket. Shiv recalled his score of 100 plus vs Bermine, a team from Berbice, in the finals at Bourda Cricket Ground. There were many others among the cricket cognoscenti at Bourda who recognized his ability and encouraged him.

Shiv has always expressed his gratitude to those who supported him (both morally and financially) – Neil Singh, President of Georgetown Cricket Club, Lester Armorgam from Trinidad, Uncle Harry Ajoda, Sheik Mohammed, Uncle Cecil Dhanraj and Uncle George (Zaheer Haniff's father). These uncles would accommodate him at nights. As an Under-16 player he had to show determination and strength of will.

During his Under-19 cricketing period (1992-93), Shiv played for Guyana's senior team. At Sabina Park, Jamaica in 1991 vs the Leeward Islands, he played under unfamiliar conditions. This only tested his resolve to succeed. The first ball delivered by Fleming, he never saw. The second was fended and that gave him some measure of confidence. Faoud Bacchus told him to "play what you see". He went on to score 75, much to the delight of a responsive spectating public. Against Barbados, he scored 40 and 70 but dehydration affected his small physical frame and he had to return to the Dressing Room. It was comforting for him as two Guyanese, Jagnarine Mohan and Anand James brought food that he liked.

In 1992, Shiv played at Bourda vs Trinidad where he achieved a century. His performances were so commendable that he was getting good recognition as a player.

Shiv's initial first class match vs the Leeward Islands at

Bourda was like a baptism of fire against the pace and guile of Kenny Benjamin. Hamish Anthony and Vaughn Walsh. He was run out for 0 in the first innings. But in his second sojourn at the crease, his courage and resilience against intimidatory bowling earned him a score of 91. He was denied a century as he ran out of partners. He was eventually bowled with an inside edge as he tried to rush to his 100. In this tournament Shiv took 20 wickets and scored over 300 runs and he was made Player of the Series.

At Albion vs Barbados, in a first class match he had one score in the 50s against intimidatory bowling and was the victim of sledging as he was warned by the Barbadians who threatened "to kill me on Barbados pitches". For him there was no lack of confidence but a strong resolve to battle against them.

As a batsman, he continued to show his mettle and was selected in the West Indies Under -19 to tour England. In the first match at Trent Bridge he scored a double century. Shiv recounts that his countryman, rice magnate and businessman, Benny Sankar was so enthused that he gifted him with $100 USD when he returned to Guyana from a travelling trip. Benny would always do this.

Back in Guyana in 1993, he played in a President Cup Match and made 140 vs Pakistan. The highlight of the match was his achievement against a strong Pakistan team comprising Javed Miandad, Salim Malik, Inzaman Ul Haq, Rameez Raja and Basit Ali. Here he also captured 4 wickets, among them, the wickets of Malik and Ul Haq. His bowling skills were most evident here as well as in the territorial matches.

Shiv continued to commit himself to achieving in club cricket and expressed his desire to be selected at the highest level of cricket. Complacency never blurred his vision nor his dream in pursuit of the highest level of performance. His enduring courage, his determination and passion spurred him on to achieve with pride and a sense of personal fulfillment. People encouraged him as they saw his potential. It led Buddy Shivraj, and his brother to gift him a car to help him as he had problems travelling to and from the grounds.

Forever will he express gratitude to those who had helped him in his pursuit. Danny Boodoo from the East Coast was of great support. The club President Jeffery Fraser took time to take him to the ground, encouraged him and got him cricket equipment. Here was a youth, magnanimous in his praise for his supporters, knowing full well their faith in his skill and ability. This inspired him to never surrender to failure but to make success a virtue. Their admiration was a compelling call to rise to the occasion when it mattered to his team.

Guided by patience and fortitude, he felt that opportunities would have presented themselves to perform for team and country and even region. His domestic career had flourished and prepared him for the "swelling act" of Test cricket. It was most exciting as well as shocking when he heard the news that David Holford, Chairman of the Selectors together with coach Rohan Kanhai, had selected him for the highest level of Test cricket. It was comforting to know that David Holford had made the call to select him in spite of resistance from others in the cricketing circle.

Chapter 3

Decline Surfaces

The 'family silver' accumulated over the years was now wasted by a 'cavalier bunch'.

Sir Hilary McD Beckles

Shiv's entry into international cricket was productive as well as exciting. The West Indian victory over England, his personal performance and contribution to team and the thrill of Lara's record-breaking event brought a sense of euphoria to the region. Shiv was part of the experience and his input contributed to the spirit of joy and thrill which pervaded. But it was also a time when the team was in a state of transition – a time when the old guard on the 70s and 80s was leaving the station and being replaced by new sentinels.

In 1994, Desmond Haynes and Richie Richardson remained. They were the only ones left from the very successful team which had reigned supreme for almost two decades. Richie Richardson was offered the captaincy role instead of Desmond Haynes who was his senior. In the period 1994-95 there was a decline in standard and performance. The team was becoming vulnerable as evident by their 1995 performances.

A visit to India in Oct – Dec 1994 was followed by a New Zealand tour in Jan – Feb 1995 and subsequently a home contest vs Australia in Mar – May 1995. That year the West

Indies struggled to maintain supremacy in world cricket. Their first Test loss to India was the first sign of decline. The records reveal that West Indies did not go beyond a 300 innings total in the first Test. Though India had a clear advantage in the second Test, their slow batting limited their chance of a second victory. However, West Indies recovered in the third Test to win by a wide margin. This meant that the series was drawn 1-1, and this brought the team spirit alive.

Test 1 India	**272**	**W.I**	**243**	**India won**
	333		**266**	
Test 2 India	**546/9**	**W.I**	**428**	**Match drawn**
	208/7		**132/5**	
Test 3 W.I	**443**	**India**	**287**	**W.I won**
	301/3		**114**	

Shiv 1 Test (4 and 11 not out)

Shiv recollects that he sat on the bench waiting his turn to be selected. He was anxious and hoped for inclusion in the Tests, but played in one Test only.

In the New Zealand Two – Test series which followed, the Kiwis demonstrated great cricketing prowess, but succumbed to the West Indies batting and bowling attack in the second Test. Here Shiv was included in the team and contributed 69 in the first innings in which West Indies accumulated 605 for 5. In the second innings he also passed

50 with a score of 61 not out. His consistency was becoming more and more obvious. The monumental West Indian total was a great task to counter and the Kiwis caved in.

Test 1	**NZ**	**341/8**	**W.I**	**312**	**Match drawn**
		61/2			
Test 2	**W.I**	**660/5**	**NZ**	**216**	**W.I won**
				122	

Shiv averaged 130.00 (1st placed)

The series did give the team hope for better days.

A return to the West Indies is 1995 to confront the Australian's was next on the agenda. The West Indies were a team that all other cricketing countries respected and they were now on home ground. Ascendency seemed assured based on their dominance over the past two decades. Players of the calibre of Lara, Hooper, Richardson, Walsh and Adams were capable of acquitting themselves when the occasion demanded. This series outcome, however, would prove disconcerting to West Indies' sensibility.

An Australia team, shorn of the services of their main pace attack, McDermott and Damien Fleming, seemed a weakened one. However, a professional approach to the game brought victory to them in the first encounter at Kensington Oval, Barbados. It was a reprieve from the 1-4 loss Australia had suffered in the One Day International preceding the Test series. The grave humiliation for the West Indies was its defeat within three days and a loss by ten wickets in the first Test. The sporting public could not reconcile the outcome of the ODIs and the Tests performances.

Test 1 W.I	**195**	**Aus**	**346**	**Aus won**
	189		**39/0**	
Test 2 Aus	**216**	**W.I**	**260**	**Match drawn**
	300/7		**80/2**	
Test 3 Aus	**128**	**W.I**	**136**	**W.I won**
	105		**98/1**	
Test 4 W.I	**265**	**Aus**	**531**	**Aus won**
	213			
	Shiv not selected			

After the rain-affected second Test, the West Indies recovered in the third Test with a victory that levelled the series 1-1. This outcome was the subject of debate as there was criticism of an unprepared pitch at the Queen's Park Oval. It incensed the Australian Press.

The last and final encounter at Sabina Park, Jamaica, was disastrous for the West Indies team. It was a crushing defeat by an innings and 53 runs, and more so, as it was 22 years since West Indies had suffered a series defeat on home ground. The defeat exposed the vulnerability which most critics had discerned over the past two years.

Inconsistent batting performances by the West Indies were countered by determined efforts from a disciplined and professional team which amassed a formidable total, doubling the West Indies first innings score. It was 265 against 531. The second innings attempt was also bereft of solidity and character as the batsmen faltered once more. In the Australian effort, neither Ambrose nor Walsh nor Kenny Benjamin, for all their fire power, was effective in disturbing the Australian onslaught, particularly the performances of both Mark and Steve Waugh. The outcome was a surrender to the more efficient team, one with resolve and stamina and purpose. After this humiliation, many began to question the future of West Indies cricket, suggesting that defeat meant fragility and vulnerability.

The critics were not enthused. Words such as 'fragile, vulnerable, lack of discipline' surfaced among the cognoscenti and, in particular, the Press and the West Indian public. Outside of the Caribbean, critics were vitriolic. One comparison likened the West Indian team to a wall which had collapsed at last. It was described as a dynasty overthrown by a relentless team. There was criticism that the West Indies were not fully motivated as in previous years and that the game had been lost in the mind.

Wisden 1995 headlined a piece "New World Change" in reporting the West Indies defeat.

"West Indies, for so long top of the Test tree, home or away, were comprehensively unseated with Australia's four-day innings victory in Jamaica. Mark Taylor's men, shorn early in the tour of two of their best bowlers (McDermott and Fleming), put the Trinidad defeat firmly behind them and took the series 2-1, inflicting on West Indies their first home series defeat for 22 years (Ian Chappell's 1972-73 Australians) and first anywhere since 1979-80, when they lost 0-1 in a contentious rubber in New Zealand. The Australian combination recaptured the Frank Worrell Trophy having used the same XI in all four Tests".

At home, there was a sense of fury revealed in the critical assessment of West Indies decline. The West Indies media sprang to life in their mocking headlines such as 'Disgraced, Overthrown' and 'Aussies Whip Windies'. There was lament, sorrow, a sense of disappointment, frustration and anger.

Harsher responses came from the series intellectual group, from Michael Manley to Hilary Beckles to Rudy Webster. Among other thinkers, there were criticisms aimed at exploring the status of West Indies cricket and the pursuit of constructive discussion in order to regain some measure of respectability to West Indian cricket.

Michael Manley, a respected voice in cricket, appealed for discussion and debate on the nature of the demise. In doing so, he raised issues of professionalism and commitment. For him, pride in performance and the sense of nationalism were fading. The flame which had ignited and illuminated West Indian cricket was becoming dimmer and dimmer.

Hilary Beckles' analysis pointed to a collapse of nationhood. The years of achievement, the harvest reaped over the years was now in decay. The 'family silver' accumulated over the years was now wasted by a 'cavalier' bunch. Later, as the decline intensified, Beckles later described it as a 'loss of soul' indicative of loss of commitment, professionalism, decay in values, mental decadence and lack of will. He envisaged a community of players with no fixed ideals but yearning for commercial gain. The greater hurt was felt because of its disparity in values and ideals – character, professionalism and discipline of most teams set against recalcitrance and lack of the positives which deny achievement and also victory.

After his debut, Shiv save for an appearance in India and in New Zealand, sat on the bench and was not selected for eight Tests which followed. He was in the midst of the failure and the commotion that spread particularly among players and the Cricket Board. This made his initiation into the cricket arena more complex than he originally felt after the first series. Here was a young initiate, having experienced the euphoria of the English series in 1994, now in the midst of conflict amidst the turbulence in West Indian cricket.

After the defeat by Australia, the West Indies team were off to England for an extended series. There, the decline continued when England captured the Texaco Trophy. In the tour later, some measure of pride was evident with a drawn Cornhill Test series. For the West Indies, a 2-2 drawn series was a reprieve.

It was only after eight (8) Tests that the West Indies selectors called up Shiv as a replacement for the injured Adams. It was also amidst the turmoil that beset the English tour in the Cornhill Test Series. This certainly was no 'climate' for the young man. On his appearance at the crease in the fifth Test his scores of 18 and 5 not out, hardly reflected his ability.

Test 1 Eng	**199**	**W.I**	**282**	**W.I won**
	208		**129/1**	
Test 2 Eng	**283**	**W.I**	**324**	**Eng won**
	336		**223**	
Test 3 Eng	**147**	**W.I**	**300**	**W.I won**
	89			
Test 4 W.I	**216**	**Eng**	**437**	**Eng won**
	314		**94/4**	
Test 5 Eng	**440**	**W.I**	**417**	**Match drawn**
	269/9		**42/2**	
Test 6 Eng	**454**	**W.I**	**692/8**	**Match drawn**
	223/4			

Shiv played 2 Tests.

Tour average 59.00 (2nd placed)

As Wisden put it, Chanderpaul "finally reclaimed his place" after an absence of eight Tests. Shiv, together with Stuart Williams and Courtney Browne, all youngsters, made favourable performances. Tony Cozier acknowledged that these youngsters' presence was encouraging for the future. When Shiv was selected for the sixth and final Test, he defined his batting role with a 'cultured' 80. Shiv played in two Tests only but his tour average was second to Lara, with an av. 59.00

In a dejected mood Shiv articulated his thoughts and feelings about the selectors' treatment of him.

In the Australian series he was relegated to the bench as there were senior players who got priority in the team. "I was the water boy but that was no problem. I was not given the chance to practise at the nets. It was only due to Adam's injury that I played in Tests 5 and 6 vs England in the series that followed."

Shiv was told by his captain, Richardson that he had to wait his turn as he was one of the younger ones. He recalls "I felt on my present performance I could have been tried more; it was a bit discomfiting for me to wait so patiently."

After his introduction to Test cricket in 1994, Shiv sat on the bench amidst the failure, dissension and conflicts. He returned to a place in the team only after the England tour had started and matches had been lost.

The following piece tells of the 'climate' of West Indian cricket during the England tour:

"During the English tour, evidence of fracture within the team was apparent and real. Unpleasantness reared its ugly head with incidents of indiscipline and perversity, all disruptive to West Indies progress. Players were disciplined by the Cricket Board. Lara and Hooper took turns to be absent for a while, and Winston Benjamin was sent home. Tony Cozier described West Indian cricket as reeling from the bombardment of negativity. There was discussion about the Board's relationship with the players.

It was noted that 'cracks' which had surfaced during the Australian tour had widened in England and the team spirit had degenerated into indiscipline. The team members no longer looked like a united team but a splintered one with struggles and internal conflicts.

With dissonance in the team, it made for disintegration which invited failure. Performance began to show its diminishing, negative effects as 1995 moved into 1996.The 'adopted' mentality carried with it a sterility and desiccation that stultified the growth of creditable cricket performance. And as players were experiencing results that damaged their sense of pride and nationhood, sterility intensified and failure mounted. As the years progressed there was an absence of fecundity, fruition, fertility and there were visible signs of failure." (Lara – The Untamed Spirit) Clifford Narinesingh.

The events of 1995 had blemished the reputation of which West Indian cricket had been proud. The failures and attendant negative outcomes affected critics, administration and spectators intensely. The sense of nationhood as evident in cricket culture was negated by the players' interest in commercialism which was growing more attractive to professional cricketers. This self-interest was a detriment to the virtues of patriotism and nationalism.

Chapter 4

Decline Continues Apace

Nothing great was ever achieved without enthusiasm.
(Essays: Circles)

The decline took a toll on the whole West Indian Cricket fraternity – Board, players, spectators. The defeat by Kenya in the World Cup 1996 series drew severe condemnation from critics and supporters. It was utter humiliation. Kenya restricted West Indies to a 93 run total. Wisden Monthly described the loss as the greatest upset in One-Day International cricket history. It was felt that complacency had caused West Indian demise. The only semblance of resistance came from Shiv (19) and Roger Harper (17).

The after effects of the loss to Kenya and the over-all failure of the team brought about serious consequences: – Andy Roberts was relieved of his position. Wes Hall indicated his unavailability for further assignments; Peter Short, WICB President, declined re-election and team captain Richardson resigned.

This defeat left spectators and fans dejected and saddened. It must not be forgotten that the audience is an integral part of the drama. Their passion, their laughter, smiles, banter and retort – all part of their support. Deep down there is that passion that stimulates them, a desire for the team's success as they share the joys of victory and the pangs of defeat. This particular loss shocked the entire Caribbean and further alienated spectator support.

With the numerous goings-on, Hilary Beckles assessed the crisis and saw the problems as more deep-seated than structural change or change in personnel. He saw a crisis emanating from poor performance and the disintegration of team leadership and managerial authority. The tension among cricket analysts was rooted in the knowledge that high standards had been diluted and more so, abandoned. What was central to the discussion was a lack of professionalism, purpose and direction as the team sank into ruins. There was a further call for more profound discussion as initiated previously by Michael Manley after the 1995 Sabina loss to Australia.

After the World Cup failure in 1996, the defeat of New Zealand in a two Test series (1-0) was a little consolation. The true test followed with encounters with Australia at the end of the year. There was the great hope to avenge the 1995 loss in the Caribbean. But Australia's' strength, on home pitches, was formidable. The West Indians lacked the resilience and mental strength and these factors were debilitating.

Test 1 NZ	**195**	**W.I**	**472**	**W.I won**
	305		**29/0**	
Test 2 W.I	**548/7**	**NZ**	**437**	**Match drawn**
	184		**130/5**	

Shiv averaged 43.66

In both Tests 1 and 2 at Brisbane Nov 22-26, 1996 and Sydney, Nov 29-Dec 3 1996, defeats were most dispiriting as Australia's dominance prevailed. Hooper was consistent and Shiv the 'arch-scorer of half centuries" was competent but the majesty of Lara was missed. Lara's failed innings yielded 26, 44, 2 and 1. In response to Australia's 479 in the first innings of the Brisbane Test, West Indies managed 277; it was a 202 deficit they had to surmount. Here Hooper and Shiv were the only combatants – a gifted century from Hooper and a combative 82 from Shiv. Both batsmen relieved the pressure from a dismal start (77 for 3) with a rescue mission which yielded a partnership of 172. Their contribution lent respectability to the total. But scores of 277 and 296 in the two West Indian innings suggested that nothing could change. The Brisbane Test concluded with a 123-run Australian victory.

Test 1 Aus	**479**	**W.I**	**277**	**Aus won**
	217/6		**296**	
Test 2 Aus	**331**	**W.I**	**304**	**Aus won**
	312/4		**215**	
Test 3 Aus	**219**	**W.I**	**255**	**W.I won**
	122		**87/4**	
Test 4 W.I	**130**	**Aus**	**517**	**Aus won**
	204			
Test 5 Aus	**243**	**W.I**	**384**	**W.I won**
	194		**57/0**	

Shiv averaged 38.22 (2nd placed)

The encounter at Sydney which followed resulted in an Australian 124-run victory. Here fortunes seemed more auspicious as West Indies trailed on the first innings by only 27 runs but later squandered an opportunity. Given 340 to challenge in just over a day, there was no resistance with the exception of Hooper and Shiv. Shiv struck back with such abandon that Shane Warne had to be removed from the attack. He reached 50 in just 38 balls and with Hooper put on 117 in a bare 95 minutes. That rate of scoring might have delivered victory. But Warne returned and "conjured a ball, that had it held its line, would have gone to slip". Instead it rounded wickedly on Shiv and cannoned from his pad into his stumps. In spite of the results, Shiv achieved the scores of 48 and 71 in this Test. The dismissal, has been considered to date, as one of the strangest.

Within an hour of Shiv's departure, Hooper fell to Michael Bevan and no other batsman offered resistance.

The Third Test at Melbourne in December 26-28, 1996 saw a change in fortune as Australia's modest scores permitted a victory that did not call for too much improvement in the batting. It was a low-scoring match. Ambrose showed signs of his former self by capturing 5 wickets in the Australian first innings and four in the second innings. In the batting it was Shiv's (58) in the first innings with good contributions from Adams (74) and Murray (53) that assured a first innings lead of 36. Ambrose then helped reduce Australia to 122 with the capture of 4 wickets. Set a total of 87 for victory, Shiv (40) and Hooper (27 n.o) saw West Indies to a 6-wicket victory. In this Test Shiv had achieved his 11th 50 in 21 Test appearances. And with this victory, West Indian enthusiasm came alive and hopes were rekindled. The victory brought to mind West Indian resurgence versus Australia in 1992/1993. With optimism and renewed energy, they looked forward to the fourth Test in Adelaide.

Adelaide, however, proved a disappointment for the West Indians. The veteran Ambrose withdrew due to injury. In his absence, there was no hope of defending a humiliating first innings score of 130. The West Indies not only succumbed to Australia's powerful bowling armoury but proved pathetic in the field. Dropped catches, a mis-stump and three no-ball wickets further demoralized the team.

In response to the West Indies' meagre 130, Australia amassed a formidable 517. A huge 387 deficit was daunting. The reply was inadequate and lusterless with only Hooper (45) and Lara (78) helping the side to stumble to 204.

There was some comfort to West Indies in the last Test at Perth which saw some sparks in West Indies bowling. A 243 dismal total gave West Indians the freedom to assert themselves and restore some honour before their departure. It was here that Lara's dominance was impressive. An "innings of power as much as imagination" was an appropriate description of his batting skills in this match.

The victory, a 10-wicket one, concluded with a 3-2 outcome but it was too late for real comfort. If West Indies were to depart from their 'losing ways' their thrust needed to be movement to greater consistency with the bat and a more varied bowling attack.

It is interesting to glean the batting averages of the key players in the West Indies. Carl Hooper was at the top – 362 runs av. 45.25, Shiv 344 runs av. 38.22, R. Samuels 231 runs av. 33.00 and Brian Lara 296 runs – average 32.88. In contrast, five Australian batsmen averaged over 40 with three of them going beyond 50. If the West Indies were to be judged by consistency, only two emerged – Hooper and Shiv.

On reflection, the series called for greater introspection, more training and most importantly, the need for loyalty and commitment. This Australian tour was labelled as a 'decider' but in spite of the pre-tour hype, it was not a game changer. In his summary of the tour, Greg Baum described the West Indies, 'wincing from their own wounds', including the knowledge that their decline as the paramount power of world cricket was continuing apace.

(L to R) Brandon, Uma, Lijana, Khemraj, Shiv, Ciara and Christopher

(L to R) Janet, Chris, Shiv

(Above L to R) Lijana, Christopher, Shiv, Ciara and Grandma.

Above (L to R) Kundan,,Krishna, Darshan and mother, Leila Chickery

Right (L to R) Darshan, Auntie Leila, Krishna, Rhada and Kundan.

(L to R) Geeta, Shiv, Devi

(L to R) Khemraj, Uma, Shiv,Devi & Geeta

Shiv and Family

(L to R) Devi, Shiv, Geeta

(L to R) Shiv, Lijana, Ciara

(L to R) Shiv & Tajenarine (Brandon)

Shiv displays his awards

Above: Shivnarine and the WI team meet Queen Elizabeth II

Shiv in a post WI players of Guyana photo. Middle row, fourth from left.

Shiv in a WI team photo, front row, third from left.

(L to R) Sunil Gavasker interviews Shiv at Queen's Park Oval (Trinidad).

Above: Shiv receives the Doctor of Laws (LLD) Honoris Causa from Chancellor Robert Bermudez(UWI).

Shivnarine arrives in India.

Shiv speaks with students at a school.

Chapter 5

Shiv's Sunshine in the Shadow

In the midst of decline Shiv scored his first century.

The prevailing mood at the end of the year, 1997, was one of despondency and utter frustration. West Indies were labelled as unpredictable. Failure and success alternated as the years progressed but failure was more dominant; victory becoming more and more remote. There were frequent references to past imperious West Indies performances and the imposing stature which had intimidated their cricketing rivals. Many recalled West Indian dominance and arrogance – an arrogance which was startling. It was evident in the ruthless performances of the four-pronged attack and exhibited particularly in Richard's stride or swagger as he emerged onto the field. But now the prevailing mood was one of sympathy for the fallen heroes.

After their failures in 1996, the West Indies hoped for brighter times and felt that the presence of Lara, Hooper and Shiv would make them at least competitive. They were now bent on greater prospects for the tours of India and Sri Lanka on home grounds, then abroad in Pakistan – all sub-continent rivals.

Test 1 W.I	**427**	**India**	**346**	**Match drawn**
	241/4		**99/2**	

Test 2 W.I	**296**	**India**	**436**	**Match drawn**
	299/6			
Test 3 W.I	**298**	**India**	**319**	**W.I won**
	140		**81**	
Test 4 W.I	**333**	**India**	**212/2**	**Match drawn**
Test 5 India	**355**	**W.I**	**145/3**	**Match drawn**

Shiv averaged 73.83 (1st placed) 1/100

In 1997, India ranked third in the International Test ranking followed by West Indies in fourth place. As with all Indian visits, there was great excitement and hope for intense rivalry. This tour promised high drama because of the magical performance of Tendulkar in the Indian team and anticipation of a Tendulkar vs Lara sub-plot. But this never happened during this tour or any other. The debate still continues about pitting the two batting legends against each other.

It was a tour disturbed by inclement weather conditions. The first, fourth and fifth Tests were interrupted by incessant rain. Though the first Test was interrupted by rain, there was always the possibility of a decisive conclusion. Set a first innings target of 427 made from the bats of Shiv (52), Lara (83) and Hooper (129), India responded with 346. The partnership between Sherwin Campbell and Shiv had all the ingredients of a formidable innings but they did not "capitalize on solid starts". After the dismissals of Campbell and Shiv, a delightful third wicket stand from Lara and Hooper provided "a sumptuous treat for the spectators – an innings fraught with finesse and aggression".

India's 346 response gave West Indies the impetus to work towards a challenging target. To advance the match for a decisive result, West Indies declared at 241 for 4. In spite of interruption, Lara and Shiv produced a partnership of 122 to attain up a total of 241. The challenge was a 322 target to accomplish in one day.

Asking India to score 322 in 90 overs was a sporting challenge but rain interruption reduced the 90 overs to a mere 53 and this made for a drawn Test. The elements denied a thrilling outcome and this was an occasion to test the resolve of both teams.

Had it not been defensive cricket in India's second innings of the second Test in Port of Spain, they might have reprised their victory at Queen's Park in 1971. However, they seemed constrained and unable to explore their chance of conquest. India had achieved a lead of 140 in response to West Indies first innings of 296. In their second effort, they accumulated 436 runs, scored off 183.4 overs. It seemed dull but in their defence, the West Indian bowling was exceedingly accurate. In response, an obdurate Shiv (79) partnered with Williams (128) to deny India any chance of victory. Tony Cozier reported that Williams and Shiv "dropped anchor until the final afternoon, ensuring there were no undue alarms."

A dramatic third Test at Bridgetown, Barbados, with strong

indications of India's path to victory concluded with a West Indian triumph. India's 319 in reply to West Indies 298 gave them a slim 21 runs lead but it was Shiv's day and his effort was a major factor in the unfolding drama. He finally achieved his first century after a series of 13 fifties in his Test career. On a difficult pitch he converted his 14th fifty to a 137 not out century. The innings was a fitting response to detractors who had questioned his ability to go the distance. His carefully structured 137 was a powerful statement. He had shown that he could dominate at the wicket.

India's pace seemed too much for West Indian bats but Shiv was resolute. They "could not dislodge Chanderpaul who entered in the third over and remained unbeaten after nearly seven and a half hours during which he struck 12 fours and offered no chance. His 137 followed a sequence of 13 scores of half centuries. His relief was evident as he kissed the pitch," an action that became a ritual every time he scored a century. This gesture had been ridiculed by the cynical Australian team but for Shiv, the pitch was perceived as the sacred and hallowed ground which brought him success in his career. It gave him self-esteem and the satisfaction that he could perform for his team and the region.

Though five wickets had fallen for 131, Shiv had crucial support from Browne and Ambrose in his fighting effort to accumulate a respectable score for the West Indies. Shiv remembers: "I played on a difficult pitch, a green seamer, lots of bounce. Everyone else had got out so I knew if we were going to reach a decent score I'd have be there to the end. I got good support from Curtly Ambrose to reach my century. When he came in, he ran everything. He encouraged me towards that century."

Each team had an equal chance at victory as they entered the second innings but a West Indian collapse to a paltry 140 gave India the freedom to smile their way to victory. With competent batsmen such as Sachin Tendulkar, Rahul Dravid, Navjot Singh Sidhu and VVS Laxman in the team, a 120 victory target was most achievable. But a sudden dramatic collapse at 52 for 6 shattered India's hopes. They capitulated with their score at 81. It was a disastrous outcome for a match which was strong in India's favour. It was a thrilling victory that West Indies would fondly remember as coming from imminent defeat. Critics cited it as another instance of the unpredictability of cricket, but it was poor batting and good bowling which caused this capitulation.

The St. John's fourth and Bourda's fifth matches were at the mercy of the elements. Nothing significant was achieved as the series petered out into dull encounters. Though West Indies emerged victorious in the series, they were not the gallant knights in shining armour of old.

A one-day International series followed the weather-ruined Test series and rain did further damage to the One-Days. The first two were reduced but both teams shared the honours 1-1. The third and fourth were in West Indies favour and the series ended with a 3-1 West Indian advantage.

In the first ODI, Shiv in the role of opener, played with confidence and vibrancy – a testament to his prolific form. His unbeaten 83 came from 87 deliveries and to his credit, 12 fours; it was exquisite timing that embellished his innings. He continued in the fourth ODI when West Indies were set a target of 199. Stuart Williams (78 n.o) and Shiv (109 n.o) wrapped up the match without a wicket's loss. It was a record partnership in West Indies ODI matches. The method of domination in the ODIs brought a freshness to the character of the batsmen. There was evidence of perfect timing and execution in Shiv's shots. It gave the spectators moments of joy and enervated their senses as they indulged in the revelry of success. The crowd was treated to delightful and entertaining cricket as both batsmen shared 25 fours. Shiv was assertive in his innings and steady as a lamp whose brilliance could not be smothered by the raging wind of pace. Based on Shiv's Test performances and his ODI success, he was awarded Man of the Series.

A two-Test series between Sri Lanka and West Indies in June of 1997 without the injured Shiv, ended with a 1-0 West Indian success. Both teams produced meagre totals unworthy of Test standards. In the first Test, West Indies won by six wickets mainly through Sri Lanka's second innings collapse. Rain affected the second Test which was proving to be an interesting one as Sri Lanka were 36 runs short of victory with two wickets in hand. Shiv was absent in this series due to a neck injury.

Test 1 SL	**223**	**W.I**	**189**	**W.I won**
	152		**189/4**	
Test 2 W.I	**147**	**SL**	**222**	**Match drawn**
	343		**233/8**	

Shiv injured

After the two visits from the Asian continent, the West Indies' scheduled visit to Pakistan took place at the end of the year. It was a much anticipated series, which it was hoped, would further enlighten the sporting public about the West Indies presence in world cricket.

The West Indians were bundled out in the first Test at Peshawar. On the first day's play they were reeling at 29 for 4 with Lara back in the pavilion, having scored 3. The innings crawled to 58 for 7. Only a rear guard effort by the tailenders took them to 151. Pakistan batting experienced no difficulty from the West Indian bowling attack and were helped by a pathetic display of fielding and dropped catches. This enabled Pakistan to accumulate a commanding 381. Facing a lead of 230, the West Indian second innings response was inadequate. They surrendered almost feebly for 211 which meant a loss by an innings and 19 runs. One of their most reliable batsman, Shiv, had failed in both innings with scores of 0 and 14. The signals mirrored atrophy and decline.

Another pathetic performance in the second Test at Rawalpindi meant there was no challenge for a series decider. A defeat by 229 runs seemed to replicate the first Test surrender.

Test 1 W.I	**151**	**Pak**	**381**	**Pak won**
	211			
Test 2 W.I	**303**	**Pak**	**471**	**Pak won**
	139			

Test 3 W.I	**216**	**Pak**	**417**	**Pak won**
	212		**15/0**	

Shiv averaged 25.50 (3rd placed after Hooper and Campbell)

The only resistance came from Sherwin Campbell (70) and Shiv (95). Shiv missed his century due to circumspect batting in the 90s and the best partnership of the series was shared by Campbell and Shiv. These two showed confidence as they added 149 to contribute to West Indies' highest total in the series. But even Shiv, with low scores in the other innings, did not measure up to expectations. The other batsmen did not impress and this appeared calamitous in the eyes of the critics.

Hooper's 73 in the second innings was inconsequential. Lara's failures mounted as he failed in both innings. Captain Walsh was dismayed by their failures and lamented: "We are beginning to look a bit pathetic and drastic action is needed." Walsh was experiencing the cold reality of defeat and was showing signs of deep frustration.

The third Test at Karachi resulted in a ten-wicket loss for West Indies. It was a whitewash, something that they did to others in their period of dominance.

The series vs Pakistan has been described as the most disastrous performance since the initiation of West Indies into world cricket. Comparisons have been made with West Indies loss to England in the 1928 series, but that was a fledgling West Indian team on their first Test assignment, doing battle with an experienced English outfit.

This 3-0 whitewash was incomprehensible to a West Indian multitude. Here was a vibrant and dynamic demonstration of Pakistan's cricket which caused humiliation to our team and people; it left a dejected Caribbean audience in dismay. The flaws in performance, mental approach and cricketing skills were most visible as Pakistan completely demoralized their rivals in every aspect of the game. West Indian frailty was exposed and there would have been no argument to save their reputation as great world class cricketers. The reaction from the West Indian cricketing fraternity revealed hurt and disenchantment.

For the management with Clive Lloyd as the flagbearer, it was doubly disappointing for him to have experienced the luxuries of victory during his years and now the pangs of defeat. With regret and a feeling of disillusionment, Lloyd lamented, "To say we are playing bad cricket is being nice to them. It is unbearable-------. We have built a reputation as fighters. Our cricket was built on purpose, application, dedication and pride, and we have lost that." The language loudly conveys hurt, disappointment, sadness and disgust at the performance, coupled with a recognition of the glorious past of West Indian impact on the game and the motivating positives of sportsmanship which inspired their presence on the cricket field.

The captain, Courtney Walsh, distanced himself from the catastrophic defeat and indicated his unwillingness to be linked with such abysmal failure. At the same time he expressed allegiance to the tradition of nationalism, pride in achievement and loyalty to the region – positives which have characterized his career. The demise or collapse as it gained momentum at this time was still viewed superficially by an establishment that saw adhocracy as the remedy.

They were never expansive and profound in their analysis of West Indies failure nor did they heed the clarion call of Michael Manley who had initiated meaningful discourse. Such a discourse was ably supported by Hilary Beckles' profound analysis of the dysfunctional nature of West Indian performance and the condition of West Indian cricket.

Chapter 6

Sunshine and Shadow

From success to disaster

The debacle of the defeat by Pakistan called for a revitalization of West Indian spirit and the desire to restore respectability in world cricket. With Lara's interest in the captaincy slot, it was felt that his installation as leader could have positive outcomes. Walsh was a frustrated captain who was not perturbed by giving up the reins of leadership. He had tried with passion and example to elevate West Indian cricket but with no great success.

Many critics welcomed Lara's appointment and anticipated some form of resurgence. On England's tour of the Caribbean in January – March 1998, it was Lara's chance to elevate West Indian cricket. The series was thwarted by unforeseen dramatic moments. The first Test at Sabina Park, Jamaica, had to be abandoned because of an imperfect pitch. After 10.1 overs played in 66 minutes, the match had to be halted due to an inadequately prepared pitch. The English who were batting bore the brunt of deliveries, harmful to their bodies. Batsmen were either dismissed with one digit figures or were physically hurt. The pitch was deemed unfit for play and the match was abandoned. The ICC still recognized it as a Test match after deliberation for several days. Wisden records "all precedent suggested that this was the only correct decision and the events which have taken place cannot be expunged".

This necessitated the move to Port of Spain to stage two Test matches. In the second Test at Queen's Park Oval, England looked in better shape but emerged with only a 23-run lead in the first innings. An aggressive response from Lara (55) and Shiv (34) seemed promising but their departure caused a collapse to a score of 191. England led by 23 runs.

Test 1 Eng	**17/3**		**Match abandoned**	
Test 2 Eng	**214**	**W.I**	**191**	**W.I won**
	258		**282/7**	
Test 3 W.I	**159**	**Eng**	**145**	**Eng won**
	210		**225/7**	
Test 4 W.I	**352**	**Eng**	**170**	**W.I won**
	197		**137**	
Test 5 Eng	**403**	**W.I**	**262**	**Match drawn**
	233/3		**112/2**	
Test 6 Eng	**127**	**W.I**	**500/7**	**W.I won**
	321			

First Test ruined by state of pitch.

Shiv averaged 34.00 1/100

After England's second innings performance of 258,

West Indies were required to post 281 for victory. At 181 for 5 there were anxious moments but Hooper (94) and David Williams (62) eased the tension with an innings of resistance, in a partnership of 129. This resulted in a win by three wickets. This victory brought relief to a team with low morale and gave them the spirit to continue with greater confidence.

Within three days the third Test was played at the same venue. The West Indian first innings started well but from 93-1 they were reduced to 159, as the batsmen were confused by the English bowlers – Caddick 5/67 and Fraser 5/40. Shiv (28) and Lara (42) were the only two batsmen who resisted after the dismissal of the opening pair. The England batsmen succumbed to West Indies with a slim 14-run lead through Ambrose 5 for 25.

This set the stage for a second innings contest to arrive at a final result but a meagre score of 210 – with contributions from Lara (47), Adams (53) and Shiv (39) – set a target of 224. Atherton (49) and Stewart (83) were resolute in their response, giving England a 3-wicket victory. This was disappointing after West Indies' second Test victory.

With the series, level at 1-1, there was the prospect of an interesting fourth Test contest in Guyana. Here Shiv's and Lara's commanding batting displays were dominant. After the dismissal of the opening pair, "Chanderpaul and Lara took control in an enterprising partnership of 159". Lara fell short of his century by seven runs but his innings flourished with two sixes and thirteen fours. Wisden reports that "Chanderpaul commanded the attention as he neared his hundred. When he reached it ten minutes before the close, he was enveloped by dozens of ecstatic Guyanese". Their hero had entertained them for six and one half hours with one six and fifteen fours, much to their delight. Shiv's 118 and Lara's 93 contributed to a total of 352.

Such revelry enhances the drama in the game and reveals the joy and elation that accompany faith in one's hero's accomplishments. It is evident throughout the sporting fraternity where there is a live audience. In the Caribbean, it reveals the spirit of a people who embrace the game and its success with the greatest of pleasure and merriment. Their physical demeanour is demonstrative of their ecstasy.

With pace and spin, England were humbled to 170. This advantage helped West Indies set a target of 379 after their second innings of 197. Again, England's counter was decimated; it gave West Indies a commanding victory by 242 runs and further boosted their confidence and team morale. Shiv emerged Man of the Match.

Shiv had the highest individual score of the match and he was enterprising with Lara after West Indies had lost two early wickets. Such performance was a hint of the West Indies team's capability to raise their level of play to its former status.

Any hope of England levelling the series in the fifth Test at Bridgetown was frustrated by a deluge that thwarted any interesting conclusion on the last day. England's performance here was remarkable. A commanding 403 was followed by their dismissal of the hosts for 262 with only three batsmen – Lambert 55, Wallace 45 and Shiv

45 going beyond 40. After England's second innings declaration, West Indies were faced with a 375-challenge but the elements disrupted a crucial ending. It seemed that the only outcome could have been an England victory or a drawn Test.

A last ditch England effort in the sixth Test was negated by their first innings score of 127. The West Indian response of 500 left England facing a 373 deficit. Their effort was not combative enough to gain any positive outcome as they were limited to 321, thus concluding in a West Indian victory by an innings and 52 runs. For England it was a 3-1 series bitter defeat.

Some critics expressed disappointment in the quality of cricketing performance during the series; yet there were others who were more optimistic that West Indian resurgence was positive. However, Atherton expressed the view that the last three Tests were "hammer-blows of misfortune for England". For the West Indies, however, there was every reason to view it as a well-deserved and well-earned series victory. For them, it was a success that would encourage greater resolve and enhance self-esteem and confidence in facing South Africa later in the year.

A sense of euphoria pervaded, as even the critics were now expressing optimism as they looked to future assignments. Lara was enthused and determined to assure the West Indian public of future successes. It was felt that a new Lara had emerged and this would motivate his team of players and inspire them to play more competitive cricket.

The token of revival did not lead to a change in fortune.

In the midst of the euphoria, there were still nagging problems in the cricket circuit. Player-Board issues remained unresolved and a crisis point was reached before the tour of South Africa began.

Negotiations were not concluded and the players revolted before the November 1998 tour. Lara and Hooper were at the centre of the crisis between the Board and players.

The following piece captures the impasse between Board and players before the tour.

"The players were seeking additional monetary remuneration for matters such as meal allowances, one-day game fixtures and security guarantees in South Africa. This particular safeguard, the players insisted on, due to the mugging of two Pakistani players on tour in South Africa the previous year. The players viewed this issue as relevant and urgent before any contractual arrangement could be finalized for the South African tour.

The impasse intensified and jeopardised the tour as both Lara and Hooper journeyed to London instead of the scheduled route to Johannesburg, where some junior team members awaited them. Some other team members joined Lara in London while negotiations were proceeding. But before the resolution was reached, the Board fined both Lara and Hooper and took a decision to penalise the other members in London with a match fee reduction.

The West Indian public looked on in dismay and anger. Reactions were extreme. It was felt that the dismissal of both leaders of the team was too draconian. There were calls for the Board to resign and for the players' reinstatement. But after much deliberation and in a compromising stance, the matter was resolved. With this reconciliation, both Lara and Hooper were reinstated before the tour proceeded. Even before bargaining began in London between the Board and the Players' Association, the President of South Africa, Nelson Mandela, intervened with the request that they proceed with the scheduled tour. As the team thrust forward to South Africa, Lara apologized for any offence the team had committed and declared his mission to be victorious." Wisden.

There was another issue which was discomfiting to the players as they were not paid for all the first class matches. It was also their grievance when they played numerous first class matches in England.

The South African crisis was a regrettable one, even humiliating. It caused President Mandela to intervene with a request that the scheduled tour proceed. Board – Players conflict broke out again in 2014 when the West Indies abandoned their tour of India due to an impasse between players and Board. This incident caused the Board of Control for Cricket in India to suffer deep financial loss. Clearly there were core issues simmering that were only partly resolved. So, after Mandela's plea, the tour proceeded but the conflict remained.

Test 1 W.I	**261**	**SA**	**268**	**SA won**
	170		**164/6**	

Test 2 SA	**245**	**W.I**	**121**	**SA won**
	195		**141**	
Test 3 W.I	**198**	**SA**	**312**	**SA won**
	259		**147/1**	
Test 4 SA	**406/8**	**W.I**	**212**	**SA won**
	226/7		**271**	
Test 5 SA	**313**	**W.I**	**144**	**SA won**
	399/5		**217**	

Shiv averaged 26.60 (3rd placed) after Jacobs 45.28 and Lara 31.00

On paper, the teams seemed well-matched for the first Test at the Wanderers Ground; neither seemed the dominant partner. The Test began on a competitive note but contrary to expectation by both critics and the public, West Indies went into rapid decline from the second innings. Their middle order batsmen failed. The performances of Lara, Hooper and Shiv were disappointing. The bowling was ineffective and the batsmen gave them nothing substantial to defend.

The first innings of 261 was a competitive response to South Africa's 268. But their second innings of 170 offered no challenge to South Africa's batting. Positive cricket and resolute batting by the South Africans, especially the middle order batsmen, saw their team to victory.

Shiv top-scored with a determined 74 but his occupancy at the crease lasted for one-third of the day. A partnership of 91 with Hooper carried the innings to 261 but a second innings of 170 placed them at the mercy of the South Africans. During the tour Lara showed some sparks of brilliance but both Shiv and Hooper did not live up to their true potential. Their performances "undermined the West Indian cause," according to Wisden's report.

Throughouttheseries, SouthAfrica'spresenceasacricketing team demonstrated unwavering, serious application and progressive combative spirit. Consistent performances, the fielding skills of Jonty Rhodes and Herschelle Gibbs and a sense of discipline and determination characterised their performance throughout the series. Their brilliant outfield cricket was in stark contrast to West Indies listless athleticism.

The West Indies' decline in the series was disastrous in all aspects of the game. The West Indies' lacklustre appearances registered scores of 121 and 141 in Test two, 198 and 259 in Test three, 212 and 271 in Test four and 144 and 127 in Test 5.

In the first Test South Africa won by 4 wickets, by 178 in the second, nine wickets in the third, 149 runs in the fourth and 351 runs in the fifth. It was an annihilation which West Indies had never anticipated on this tour. It seemed atrophy, mental and physical, had worn down West Indies' impulse to combat with positive energy and spirit.

The trio of established batsmen registered the following statistics as part of their cricketing resume:

Lara – 11, 7, 4, 39, 51, 79, 4, 33, 68, 14

Shiv – 74, 1, 4, 16, 4, 75, 6, 5, 38, 43

Hooper – 44, 34, 15, 8, 10, 2, 86, 20, 8, 10

The numbers tell a story of under-achievement – an incredible performance or lack of it that negated any positive path to a creditable response to South Africa's challenge. A humiliating 5-0 whitewash and the subsequent 5-1 ODIs loss were terrible blows to both players and public who were elevated in stature a series ago before the team's show of their supremacy over England.

There were several discourses on the outcome of the series but mainly indignation pointed at the root cause – disunity, discord and arrogance which prefaced the series and the turmoil during the series. From being the cynosure of all eyes, Lara became the villain. He was chastised not only for his rebellious attitude pre-tour but also his abysmal failure as a batsman. An average 31 was condemned with cynicism. Lara reflected on the West Indies' performance and said it was his 'worst tour' and they were not together as a team.

The disaster led Alan Donald, the South African paceman, to cruelly comment on the lack of dynamism and professionalism of a young side 'out of depth'. Critics thought there was no defence that could be made as the tour had proved a disaster.

Though there was unfavourable assessment of his role as captain, Lara was assigned to lead the team in the first two

Tests against Australia. And in this new series, fortunes fluctuated with West Indies regaining some measure of pride after the South African defeat.

Chapter 7

The Trauma of Defeat

On a darkling plain with no certitude

inspired by Dover Beach (Matthew Arnold)

As the years progressed towards the end of the century, fortunes fluctuated. After the Pakistan defeat, there was victory against England, defeat by South Africa and then a drawn series with Australia at home.

The early 1999 series, (March-April) experienced a resurgence in West Indian cricket. But the pendulum of reportage revealed a blend of cynicism and euphoria as the series progressed. Australia were victorious in the first Test winning handsomely by 32 runs, but thereafter West Indies victories in the second and third Tests brought relief and optimism. However, Australia rallied on to draw the series 2-2. The first Test was demoralizing after the previous defeats. Lara was a shattered man of 'dissolution and distress' and was not spared the rage of the critics, especially Michael Holding.

If sympathy emerged towards West Indies, it was due to Shiv's absence through his shoulder injury which required treatment abroad and Carl Hooper's absence from the first two matches.

Chanderpaul off to New York for test

Bridgetown, Barbados, CANA – Injured West Indies batsman Shivnarine Chanderpaul was leaving the Caribbean last night for New York where he will have further tests on his damaged right shoulder.

The West Indies Cricket Board (WICB) said a decision was taken to send the slimly-built Chanderpaul to a New York hospital for more tests after he failed a fitness examination prior to Friday's start of the third Test against Australia.

WICB's Chief executive Officer Steve Camacho said the move was "a precautionary measure taken by the Board".

Camacho said the WICB had offered to send Chanderpaul to New York for treatment two weeks ago but the Guyanese Cricket Board had indicated that he was approaching full fitness following consultation with the WICB medical team in Guyana.

"Therefore it was felt that it was not necessary for him to go to New York at that time," added Camacho.

Eventually, the Board in good faith sent him for therapy.

During this tour, Shiv received therapy in New York but returned to Guyana where he continued treatment with Monica Benn to repair his shoulder injury.

During the series in the first Test, at Queen's Park Oval, Port of Spain, Australia put to shame the team. Facing a total of 364, West Indies were limited comfortably to a humiliating 51, their lowest total in their cricketing performance.

However, the second Test at Sabina Park, Jamaica and the third Test at Kensington Oval, Barbados saw a dramatic turn to the series, an indication of the unpredictability of West Indies' cricket performance. The second Test concluded with a 10- wicket victory for West Indies bolstered by Lara's and Adams' fortitude. His double century was a shining example of Lara's majesty at the wicket.

Test 1 Aus	**269**	**W.I**	**167**	**Aus won**
	261		**51**	
Test 2 Aus	**256**	**W.I**	**431**	**W.I won**
	177		**3/0**	
Test 3 Aus	**490**	**W.I**	**329**	**W.I won**
	146		**311/9**	
Test 4 Aus	**303**	**W.I**	**222**	**Aus won**
	306		**211**	

Shiv absent - injury

Such a sterling performance buoyed up their optimism but was countered by Australia's counter-attack. A target of 308 for victory appeared insurmountable when West Indies were struggling at 105 for 5 but once again Lara, with support from Adams and the tail, lifted the score beyond 308 with one wicket to spare. Lara's century of 153 has been hailed as one of the greatest innings ever played.

Having surpassed Australia at this point in the series, West Indies' euphoria spread across the Caribbean. However, Australia's determination and arrogance did not deter them from the battle scene. They fought back in the last Test in a competitive mood and this earned them a victory that squared the series.

The outcome, though West Indies were denied the series victory, was viewed as a resurgence – a symbol of hope and unity in a fractured and dispirited Caribbean.

Hilary Beckles in his exploration of West Indies condition and circumstances did view the performance as a symbol of the possibility for the region to enter the future with confidence and a sense of vitality.

The pattern of unpredictability in West Indian performance had become more and more evident. Though the World Cup was a disappointment, the series vs New Zealand in December 1999 was expected to elevate West Indian performance. However, a disappointing display was a 5-0 loss in the ODIs and 2-0 loss in the Tests (a complete whitewash) were disastrous. A completely annihilated team – from captain to administration – created a void. Lara expressed his agony by resigning and requested leave and the psychotherapist, Dennis Waight also resigned.

Test 1 W.I	**365**	**NZ**	**393**	**NZ won**
	97		**70/1**	
Test 2 NZ	**518/9**	**W.I**	**179**	**NZ won**
			234	

Discourse among critics focused on Lara's captaincy and West Indies cricket. Though overcome and trampled on by New Zealand team, the tour to England was scheduled for the summer of 2000 with Jimmy Adams at the helm. There was some measure of hope as Lara had decided to join the party to England for the summer tour.

The trauma of New Zealand's annihilation was discomfiting especially as West Indies' performance had always matched the efforts of New Zealand. "Onward courage, onward" was the theme of the England summer tour of the Cornhill Series when Adams continued in the leadership role. Their challenge to England began on a positive note. An innings and 93-run victory for the West Indies was great consolation for a team in decline. The batting performances of Campbell's 59, Chanderpaul's 73, Adams' 98 and Lara's 50 were a solid response to England's 179. This enthusiasm was sustained with pace bowling that limited England to a mere 125. It was a victory that demonstrated the maturity of a team which should never have waned.

Test 1 Eng	**179**	**W.I**	**397**	**W.I won**
	125			
Test 2 W.I	**267**	**Eng**	**134**	**Eng won**
	54		**191/8**	
Test 3 W.I	**157**	**Eng**	**303**	**Match drawn**
	438/7		**80/1**	
Test 4 W.I	**172**	**Eng**	**272**	**Eng. won**
	61			

Test 5 Eng	**281**	**W.I**	**125**	**Eng won**
	217		**215**	

After Test 2, Shiv injured

Shiv's Tour average 69.66 2/100s 1/50

The victory was described as "a clinically efficient win in the first Test. Victory by an innings and three days of Caribbean –like sunshine suggested West Indies supremacy was not diminished".

The second Test provided drama particularly at the end. A paltry 267, though discouraging, was heartening when West Indies pacemen Ambrose and Walsh in a fiery spell reduced England to 134, thus gaining a lead of 133. Sadly a complacent and uncompetitive display saw West Indies slumped to their lowest total in Test cricket – 54.

Though they were only chasing a target of 188, England did not have it all their own as West Indies pacers did not give up. A steadfast display of 95 for 2 saw a plunge to 140 for 6 but with defiance and intense application, England achieved their victory mission, thus levelling the series 1-1 at the conclusion of the second Test.

The other Tests which followed concluded in a 3-1 defeat for West Indies but most discouraging was the West Indies crumbling to 61 in the fourth Test. It was their second double digit total of the series. Wisden reports that the tour ended in ignominious fashion – a collapse of 61 and their first two day defeat in 70 years. A tired, dispirited West Indies surrendered the Wisden Trophy. The performances of Lara and Adams were disappointing and one key player, Shiv, was missed after tendonitis of the right shoulder ended his tour.

The tour was interspersed with a series of ODI's and first class matches and it is interesting to note that in the first class match averages for that tour, Shiv – with a total of 418 and a highest score of 161 not out – topped the tour averages with 69.66.

Despite the decline and sense of dejection, West Indies had no choice but to move positively to the next encounter with Australia in Nov/Dec of 2000. Buoyed by the faithful allegiance of supporters and determined support from all the crew involved in the administration of cricket, West Indies moved forward with renewed faith as they toured the Australian continent.

The reality of facing a formidable team on their home ground was a challenge that required use of skill and a positive outlook. The first Test at Brisbane was inauspicious with a dismal performance of 82. This was their 3rd double digit total in the past five Tests.

Test 1 W.I	**82**	**Aus**	**332**	**Aus won**
	124			
Test 2 W.I	**196**	**Aus**	**396/8**	**Aus won**
	173			
Test 3 W.I	**391**	**Aus**	**403**	**Aus won**
	141		**130/5**	

Test 4 Aus	**364**	**W.I**	**165**	**Aus won**
	262/5		**109**	
Test 5 W.I	**272**	**Aus**	**452**	**Aus won**
	352		**174/4**	

Shiv played one Test.

Mc Grath's penetrative bowling exposed the fragility of the West Indies batting. There was no imperious response to 332 with a second innings humiliating 124. It was only Shiv, in defiance of the Australian attack who produced a hard earned 62 not out in an innings of 124 runs.

As the tour progressed, West Indies became more non-combative. The second Test went to Australia but Lara's resurgence in the third Test was significant. He challenged with aggression but to no avail though with strong support from Gayle, Campbell, Hinds, Adams and Sarwan. One who could have made a difference i.e. Shiv was suffering from stress fracture and was out of the series. The fourth and fifth Tests completed the whitewash. The cynicism and scathing tone of critics was dispiriting and venomous. Steve Waugh's candid comments were condemnatory and dismissive:

"This wasn't how Test cricket is supposed to feel. I hated the lack of spirit by their team, their weak surrender, the scarcity of confrontation. Except for the heart and soul of Courtney Walsh, the talent of Brian Lara and the pluck of Jimmy Adams, they were spineless and not much better than an outfit in Sydney first-grade cricket. It's the way you win – the blood, sweat and tears that go into a hard fought victory that invigorates me, not the demolition of a non-believing foe."

Waugh's description of the West Indians as non-believing, as spineless, with lack of spirit and the will to conquer aptly portrayed a team which lacked faith in itself, a team bereft of courage and national pride. There was no semblance of a group willing to contest and express resolve to fight with courage and purpose. The West Indians looked like battle-weary troops at the point of surrender. The sense of urgency to perform had been lacking on the previous English tour before Australia; it further expressed itself as a diminishing force.

It was hoped that the disasters suffered at the hands of England and Australia would be mitigated by South Africa's visit to the islands. The comfort of home ground has often been an advantage.

After Walsh, came Lara, then Adams and nothing noteworthy changed. The Board decided to insert Hooper at the helm – known for his prowess as a batsman and an ability to spin bowl. It was felt that Hooper had the maturity to lead the team.

The series was of interest for West Indies revival – a first drawn Test, defeated in the second, drawn in the third, defeated in the fourth but coming back to win the last which concluded 2-1, a South African victory series.

West Indies revival had become the issue after defeats by England, Australia and South Africa. Their major contenders, Lara and Hooper, were flanked by youngsters

Gayle, Samuels and Sarwan – players of promise. The absence of Shiv made life more difficult.

Test 1 W.I	**304**	**SA**	**332**	**Match drawn**
	333/7		**142/2**	
Test 2 SA	**286**	**W.I**	**342**	**SA won**
	287		**162**	
Test 3 SA	**454**	**W.I**	**387**	**Match drawn**
	197/9		**88/7**	
Test 4 SA	**247**	**W.I**	**140**	**SA won**
	215/7		**240**	
Test 5 W.I	**225**	**SA**	**141**	**W.I won**
	301		**255**	

Two Tests – Shiv

The analysis was strong and vitriolic – team indiscipline, lack of application and determination, and the absence of a professional approach to the game. It was, in essence, described as tragic – no passion, no nationalistic fervour.

Chapter 8

Unfavourable Responses

The descent beckons as the ascent beckoned.

William Carlos Williams

Amidst the ongoing fluctuations that battered the team's spirit, schedules were still in place. Tours to Sri Lanka and Pakistan (at Sharjah), followed by the hosting of India and New Zealand and the West Indies return visit to India were arranged. These tours again marked fluctuations in performances but revealed much more vulnerability in the team's efforts. In the five Test series against four opponents, West Indies were rather fortunate to ease through the last Test against India on home ground to win 2-1 but India avenged their defeat on home ground later in the year. All other series ended in defeat. Victories gained in the ODI's were of little significance.

It is pertinent for the reader to peruse in some detail the performances of the teams in our analysis of West Indian response to their opponents.

This visit to Sri Lanka at the end of 2001 was disastrous for the West Indies. Notable among the absentees vs Sri Lanka was Shiv because of a back injury.

The series with Sri Lanka was a good indicator of West Indian demise. It was only Lara's competence supported by Hooper and Sarwan that was evident. However, their performances set against the might of Sri Lanka did not earn them a more respectable outcome. A whitewash seemed inevitable as both areas of batting and bowling were sub-standard. Lara's achievement was of heroic stature but a collective performance of the team members was absent. Being away from home made it even more disheartening with such under-achievement. A lacklustre spirit pervaded and this was inimical to the team's progress.

Test 1 W.I	**448**	**SL**	**590/9**	**SL won**
	144		**6/0**	
Test 2 SL	**288**	**W.I**	**191**	**SL won**
	224/6		**190**	
Test 3 W.I	**390**	**SL**	**627/9**	**SL won**
	262		**27/0**	

Shiv injured

The encounters with Pakistan followed in Sharjah. Sharjah was the alternative site following the fear of terrorism in Pakistan which had previously caused abandonment of tours. Once again the lack of collective play and achievement ran counter to positive performance. All the matches were either marred by flawed batting or substandard fielding. In the two Test matches Pakistan gained the advantage, dominating in both Tests. The three ODIs concluded with a 2-1 loss to Pakistan. Having lost the first two ODIs, West Indies achieved a consolation victory with a solid partnership between Hooper 112 not out and Shiv 67 in the third.

In the second Test match, batting, bowling and fielding were flawed and this failure was inexcusable. Such barren stagnancy that prevailed was a reflection of both mental and physical desiccation; it reflected ennui and the spirit of indolence.

Test 1 Pak	**493**	**W.I**	**366**	**Pak won**
	214/6		**171**	
Test 2 Pak.	**472**	**W.I**	**264**	**Pak won**
	225/5		**189**	

This weakness revealed of a dispirited, down-trodden team, unable to sustain strength against teams that, by reputation, were not superior to the West Indies. However, it revealed the progressive intent and performance of the sub-continent teams.

The defeats by these two sub-continent rivals were more unpalatable to West indian sensibility than bythe other giants of the game - Australia and South Africa.

The Indian tour to the Caribbean was scheduled for April of 2002. It would have given the West Indies some comfort after their Asian tour. West Indies found comfort by winning 2-1.

In the first Test in Georgetown, a docile pitch produced prodigious scores before rain washed out the final day and a half. Guyanese spectators felt proud viewing the partnership between two home-spun idols, Hooper and Shiv who chalked up the highest scores in the Tests.

West Indies didn't commence convincingly. They were 44 for three, all to Srinath, when umpire Harper gave out Lara for a duck – claimed to be caught behind by Dasgupta off a ball which seemed to have totally eluded the bat.

Hooper had managed to make 222 and 149 not out for Guyana in the knockout-stages of the Busta Shield and here he achieved a double century. Shiv and Hooper batted on for six hours and eleven minutes, adding 293. Shiv had struck 23 fours when he succumbed shortly before tea on the second day. In the next over, Hopper converted his first Test century to a double century on his home ground, after which Kumble dismissed him.

It was a memorable start to the series as the two home-grown boys were empathetic in their display as they contributed to a formidable 501 – (Hooper's graceful 233 and Shiv's 140). Wisden refers to Shiv's century as a turning of the corner for him. It was only the third time in his eight-year career that he had converted his 50s to centuries. Hooper was elegant but Shiv packed a fair punch, particularly on the drive. Of the three centurions in the match it was remarked, "If Hooper was Casanova and Chanderpaul the Processor, then Dravid was the Knight".

India suffered the loss of two quick wickets but Tendulkar lost no time in getting into the groove and began to carve an innings with a reportoire of boundaries in his inimitable style as he expressed his intention to dominate. He struck 13 fours on the way to 71 in 95 balls. Then he got reined in by Nagamootoo who confined him to eight runs in his next 41. Trying to escape the tight bind, he miscued on a pull off Mahindra Nagamootoo and was lbw at 79. Laxman remained unperturbed by this. He seemed to easily hold sway in a stand of 119 with Dravid but when Laxman was the first of the three wickets to fall within the fourth morning's five overs, India were still 27 away from saving the follow on. Earlier, Dravid on 59, despite being hit on his helmet's grill, pressed on grittily to his tenth Test hundred. He batted for seven hours and fifteen minutes, hitting 23 fours before the rain descended in furious bursts. With Sarandeep's support he ensured that there would be no further cause for concern.

On the first day of the second Test, at the Queen's Park Oval, Port of Spain, despite winning the toss, Hooper chose to bowl. West Indies had India at 262 for four. After a tentative start, Tendulkar steadied himself and scored his 29th Test hundred. Dravid seemed the more impressive performer in the partnership at 124. Tendulkar added only four on the second morning and ended his six-hour stay. It was not one of his more prolific centuries but was meaningful for the team. Then the descent set in and the final half dozen tumbled for 63. Laxman was not out at 69.

West Indies were making a very reasonable response at 179 for 4 with a vintage Lara at the crease. Then, as it was waxing late, three wickets fell for one run in ten balls. Hooper fought valiantly for three hours but received scant assistance next morning as India gained a lead of 94.

They were 56 for four when Sandford dismissed Tendulkar with his fourth ball without him scoring but Ganguly and Laxman batted through to the close and an hour in the fourth day, adding 149 to re-establish the balance.

The new ball caused it to tilt once more. When Laxman misplayed Dillon into his stumps, the remaining half dozen wickets fell for 13 runs in ten overs.

West Indies required 313 for an improbable win. Williams went early and Gayle came off because of cramp but Sarwan and Lara appeared set to see out the day. They had added 57 when Sarwan flicked a straight ball from Harbhajan Singh to slip. Soon afterwards, bad light put an end to play.

Lara was hopeful that he would convert his overnight 40 to a first Test hundred on his home turf before a huge supportive home crowd. He signalled to his local fans in the stand to lessen the level of noise – a sign perhaps of his own nervousness – and spent an uncharacteristic hour adding seven before Nehra's fourth ball of the day sent him back to the pavillion. Hooper pulled to mid-wicket in Nehra's next over and the Indians erupted in rapture.

Shiv and the returning Gayle kept them anxiously waiting just over a couple of hours for their next wicket. The stand conjured up 73 amid increasing tension. At 237, Gayle's agressive drive offered a catch to cover. West Indies needed 76 but Shiv couldn't find support to help him reach more than half way. His debacle should have ceased four overs after tea when he was deemed by the third umpire not caught behind. He was still batting nine overs later on 67 when at last Cuffy was caught at gully to give India their long-awaited first-Test win. His top score of 67 emphasized his readiness to defy the attack with Gayle's support. India won by 37 runs.

In the third Test, played at Kensington Oval, Barbados, Dillon bowled Das with the first delivery of the day and, as a result, the Indian team got that certain mentally disadvantaged feeling from the start. They were dismissed at 102 just after tea on a rain-affected first day. The pitch was encouraging and in eminently playable shape, so it was their careless stroke-play against spirited bowling that produced this paltry score. Tendulkar was out to the second ball from Collins. Ganguly was the only one who displayed some determination and combative spirit. He was at last out when Dillon followed up his four wickets with a miraculous catch at third-man boundary.

A century-stand between Lara and Sarwan gave West Indies the lead with the loss of two wickets but when Nehra took both of them in 8 deliveries, Hooper and Shiv felt compelled to restore the innings momentum. Hooper got the benefit of a run-out call at 15. An hour and a half into the third day, he was still at the crease when he hit out at Harbhajan and sent a high catch to extra cover, by which time he had put on 215 with Shiv – their second double-century partnership of the series. Shiv was 91 when he lost Hooper. The lower order collapsed. Despite this, Shiv was able to reach a hundred, which took just over six hours.

Shiv recalled that he saw the necessity to establish a total that would defy or counter any postive response by the Indians.

The visitors were in arrears by 292. Das and Jaffer put up 80. It took a direct hit from Shiv from point to separate them a little before tea and three more wickets were down by the end of the third day. West Indies required only four overs the following morning to break the stand as Collins enticed Laxman into an edge. Thereafter, only Zaheer Khan's audacious run-a-ball 46 and another determined but futile innings from Ganguly, propelled the match into a fourth afternoon and forced West Indies to bat a second time. When Dillon bagged his eighth wicket, they needed to score only five runs to level the series.

India's poor showing in the first innings of this third Test was a recipe for disaster. In contrast, the Hooper - Shiv combined execution was similar to their first Test 150 partnership in Guyana. Here was another exhibition that gave pleasure to West Indian supporters – (Shiv 101 not out and Hooper 115). This was Shiv's third century in the space of three weeks. Wisden Asia noted that "at No. 6 he can be a frustrating little chap for any opposition to run into." This partnership contributed to a 294-run score. What emerged here were the achievements of both Hooper and Shiv in championing West Indies cause with consistencey in their partnership and individual centuries.

In the fourth Test, Hooper won the toss but opted to field. Das didn't take long to lose his wicket. Tendulkar fell to his first ball off Collins. Yet India were still favourably positioned after the first day due to a stand of 155 between Dravid and Jaffer. There was some early unsteadiness when a couple of wickets fell in the space of 24 runs, including Kumble who kept on batting for four hours after a blow from Dillon left him spitting blood. Laxman took twenty two balls to get into stride. After that, however, he quickly came into his own, while Ratra kept expressing his audacious spirit as the bowling became harmless. They added

217 for India's seventh wicket, batting through to the third morning when Laxman stepped on to his off-stump from a Dillon delivery.

West Indies were not dismayed by India's 513at the St. John's Ground, Antigua, home of the fourth Test. They responded with 629 and the match ended in a tame draw. But here again Hooper's 136 and Shiv's 136 not out together with Jacob's 118, defied India's bowling. It was another Shiv- Hooper 150 partnership, making it their third 150 partnership in a series.

Hooper and Shiv had both achieved their third centuries of the series. Hooper took 401 minutes and 278 balls over his 136. Shiv copped the same score but he took 675 minutes and 510 balls. On this languid last day, Jacob provided comic relief to the crowd with the quickest match-century, completed in 172 balls. Shiv's stay at the crease catapulted him past Jacques Kallis's record of 1,241 minutes without Test-dismissal set earlier in the season. He was still there when both captains decided to call it quits.

In the fifth Test, at Sabina Park, Jamaica, Ganguly won the toss but chose – much to his later chagrin – to bowl on the lush Sabina Park pitch. This gave rise to an opening, productive partnership of 111 between the two Jamaican left handers, Gayle and Hinds. Only briefly, did West Indies relinquish their grasp.

The Indians had to wait till eight post-lunch overs to get their first wicket when Zaheer got Gayle and till midway through the final season to get their second, as Hinds added 135 more with Sarwan. However, India came back into contention with three late wickets, beginning with Hinds being caught at long-off. He had struck 14 fours and two sixes, having batted for five hours. India's retaliation continued the following morning when Srinath dismissed Hooper but then Shiv and Jacob in a partnership added 109. Wisden reports that Shiv had extended his record for batting without being dismissed to 1,513 minutes, spread out over four Tests, before Srinath ultimately defeated him.

With India set a total of 422, Dillon dismissed Jaffer and Dravid inexpensively. Tendulkar and Das added 69 and then got out within two runs of each other. And, as soon as Dillon ended the partnership between Ganguly and Laxman in the third morning, the customary collapse occurred. The last six fell for forty-four.

Despite being 210 ahead, Hooper did not enforce the follow-on but West Indies over-confidence led to laxity. They were 122 for seven when Dillon, swiping carelessly, was clean bowled by Nehra. It took diligent and careful batting from Shiv and Collins to present an unbeatable target. When Collins was out on the fourth morning, India needed to make 408 to emerge triumphant. Shiv had scored 59.

Collins removed both openers in the first two overs but Tendulkar was in such a dominant mode that the task at hand seemed somehow within reach. He scored 86 out of 145 while he was at the crease. Six balls after the tea interval, Collins, (the thorn in his flesh), bowling round the wicket, penetrated his defence to strike the middle and off. His departure knocked the wind out of the India's sails. They began to feel uncomfortable. Ganguly and Laxman both came to grief through ther recklessness. On the last morning, the tail-enders took the destined trip to futility. Shiv was the Man of the Match.

India's hope of victory in the series was ruined through a poor display of batting. Good performances from Gayle, Hinds and Sarwan followed by Jacob's 59 and Shiv's 58 saw West Indies to 400 plus. Even in the second innings Shiv's 59 demonstrated his refusal to budge, finding an unlikely partner in Pedro Collins as the lead swelled to over 400. India's task looked forbidding even with Tendulkar's efforts.

After two failures, West Indies performance at home vs India brought some re-assurance to the team. The second Test belonged to India but there was great delight when West Indies fought back to assume dominance over the Indians by winning the series 2-1. The pain of ignominy after their sub-continent tour was now replaced by moments of adulation for their successes.

Test 1 W.I	**501**	**India**	**395/7**	**Match drawn**
Test 2 India	**339**	**W.I**	**245**	**India won**
	218		**275**	
Test 3 India	**102**	**W.I**	**394**	**W.I won**
	296		**5/0**	
Test 4 India	**513/9**	**W.I**	**629/9**	**Match drawn**
Test 5 W.I	**422**	**India**	**212**	**W.I won**
	197		**252**	

Shiv averaged 140.50 3/100s 3/50s Man of the Series

In the ODI series which prefaced the Test series vs. New-Zeland, the last match produced tension and excitement at the St.Vincent ground on June 6th 2002. Set a total of 291, West Indies responded with the right temperament as they got close to the target. In the last over they need 15 for victory. At this juncture, Shiv who had suffered a blow to his arm from Bond's bowling had returned from an x-ray to continue his innings. At the wicket Shiv achieved the phenomenal finish. In this final ODI (5th), West Indies sealed the series in the last ball amid "confusion and controversy". There seemed to be a mix-up in Flemming's choice of bowler.

The first 2 balls of the last over yielded 2 runs – 1 run and 1 bye. With four balls to go and 13 needed, Shiv struck 3 fours and achieved the phenomenal finish with a single of the last ball. The camera showed the balls progress to the boundary was aborted by the uncontrollable crowd.

Test 1	**NZ**	**337**	**W.I**	**107**	**NZ won**
		243		**269**	
Test 2	**NZ**	**373**	**W.I**	**470**	**Match drawn**
		256/5			

New Zealand's first Test victory in the Caribbean in their 12th match was an all-embracing one which finished inside four days. Wisden reports it was particularly satisfying for Fleming whose first-day century underpinned his 17th Test win as captain.

The outcome was all over, bar the shouting by the second afternoon when West Indies' capricious batsmen collapsed for 107. They 'conceded' a first-innings-lead of 230. Fleming didn't enforce the follow-on.

On the first afternoon, Fleming had to lead New Zealand out of their own middle-order slump when 4 wickets fell for 29. Hart, the wicket-keeper, lent important support in a stand of 108, as Fleming completed his fourth Test hundred. He top-edged a cut to slip nine overs from the close. Hart survived to add another 112 for the last four wickets, guaranteeing a solid total.

Set a target of 337, the West Indies had their work cut out. Gayle and Sarwan fell to successive balls from Bond. Only Shiv was inclined to show some resistance. He wielded the bat for just over two hours before running out of partners. Apart from Lara who played on to Vettori, all the wickets were caught, almost all of them from attempting attacking shots. A paltry 107 was most uninspiring.

Fleming elected to bat again. But at 88 for five a victorious target seemed remote. New Zealand seemed to be loosing the commanding lead which could bring victory. But then Astle, with a flurry of strokes, achieve a 77 innings score. Astle and Flemming established a challenging target of 474, making it difficult for the West Indies.

A target of 473 seemed formidable and West Indies were challenged to achieve this in two days. In response, though, Gayle, Wavell Hinds and Lara fought bravely, the team surrendered, losing by204 run on the fourth day. Shiv was still there on 35.

Hooper won the toss in the second Test but chose to bowl. A 123 run-partnership between Richardson (95) and Astle (69) was significant and this was bolstered by Scott Styris 107. A 373 target was respectable.

The West Indian response hinged on Gayle's dam-bursting double-hundred. It featured strokes of superhuman power, including huge sixes off Butler and Bond, and four consecutive fours. During Gayle innings he partnered Sarwan in a 100 run stand and Shiv in a 143 one.

Richardson and Vincent wiped off the 97 run deficit but was then at the mercy of the spinners who claimed five wickets for forty runs on a pitch that showed signs of aging. But then Styris and Hart dismissed any thought of victory for the West Indies. A 1-0 New Zealand victory was disheartening for the West Indies.

Amit Varma and Utpal Shuvro commented that the West Indies "decline in the 1990s had accelerated into an alarming free-fall. Of the last 27 overseas Tests the West Indies had lost 23, and they had just suffered a humiliating home defeat by New Zealand.

In the ensuing series later in the year 2002, on the West Indian return, India's revenge was almost surgical. In the first Test, India won by an innings and 112 runs. The Indians were ignited, "eager to banish the demons of losing in the Caribbean earlier that year". India's achievement here in India was described as an "overwhelming team performance". They excelled in every department with an intensity in stark contrast to their opponents.

Test 1 India	**457**	**W.I**	**157**	**India won**
			188	
Test 2 W.I	**167**	**India**	**316**	**India won**
	229		**81/2**	
Test 3 India	**358**	**W.I**	**497**	**Match drawn**
	471/8			

Shiv averaged 65.00 (1st placed) 1/100 1/50

In the first Test, India got off to a positive start with Bangar playing patiently and compact when Sewhag got into gear. His 147 off 206 deliveries was built on twenty four 4s and three 6s. A significant milestone in this innings was Dravid's 4th consecutive century, one behind Everton Weekes' record of five consecutive centuries. It was a blend of both elegance and orthodoxy.

A total of 457 met no serious challenge. At 59 for 4, it was the combined efforts of Hooper and Shiv that pointed to a recovery for a while but Zaheer and Kumble soon put to rest the West Indies progress. A follow-on followed with West Indies 300 behind. At this juncture, Harbhajan Singh and Anil Kumble dominated, taking all their wickets for 188. Shiv lost company and remained on 36 not out. In the first innings, he was the last man out and he was still standing as the second innings closed.

Shiv averaged 89 in this match and was not threatened by the spinners. Wisden reports: "With an ungainly shuffle across the wicket, he played the ball late, with soft hands and perfect balance, and neutered the bowling instead of diminishing it. In this game he was a near immoveable object, batting 6 ½ hours."

After the first Test, Rahul Bhattacharya was critical of West Indies frailty and lack of professionalism.

"The West Indies ineptitude cannot be played down. Twenty-two losses in 26 overseas Tests do not occur without exceptional indifference. Allegiance to team's cause, appreciation for their own skills, there seemed to be no place for either in their cricket. The fielding was disgraceful...... The batting was poorer still. There were those who pursued the wrong strategy. There were those who got suckered... and there were those who were plain incompetent.

The bitter comment on West Indian ineptitude focused on a team stuck in a vicious circle where every loss eroded their self-esteem while their lack of self-belief kept them losing games".

Apart from Test three, the West Indies were spiritless on the field, the batting was irresponsible and the bowling lacked energy. Hooper, in commenting on the state of the second game started, "It's a shame we've come to this level." He added, "We didn't play cricket." Again in this second Test, West Indies' disastrous batting, lacklustre bowling and uninspired fielding brought their downfall. It became India's first series victory over the West Indies in twenty-four years. In response to West Indies' 167, India progressed to 316, a lead of 149. At the end of the match, India needed less than 90 to complete victory.

It is interesting to note that pollsters rating had showed

a 54% optimism that India would defeat the West Indies in four days. This was indicative of India's confidence in their players.

Gavaskar's comment was frank and compassionate, especially as everyone respected his opinion on West Indies cricket. "It's sad to see the former World Champions in such disarray but more than technique it is the mental area they need to work on to ride out the bad times. They have to tackle it quickly or else the team will become farcical and a no contest."

It was an interesting conclusion to a series though the third match ended in a draw. The West Indies as unpredictable as always, were now a determined team after two defeats. It brought back memories of the 5-1 drubbing of Clive Lloyd's team in 1975 by Australia.

In the third Test, in response to India's 358, Gayle and Hinds in a determined effort produced a 172 partnership to retrieve some pride in the series. They were combative against the spin of both Harbhajan Singh and Anil Kumble.

It was then Shiv and Samuel who continued gracefully. Shiv progressed from a quite sedate start but built with a 'blast'. His comfort against spin was not unusual as he struck 24 fours and a six in Kumble's overs and also contained Harbhajan's spin.

In the process, Shiv equalled his highest Test score (140). Samuel also proved the ideal partner with his calm demeanour but also blossomed gracefully with great elegance and command as he at times demonstrated when in good spirit. Samuel's Test century was assured. A total beyond 497 would have been more adequate if the last five batsmen had not surrendered within an hour. The lead was only 139.

However, the match seemed well poised when India slumped to 49 for 3 before lunch, due to dubious umpiring decisions.

Then with a lead still not erased and with six wickets to conquer (87-4), the match assumed dramatic intensity. Tendulkar had not been prolific in the series thus far, so he had to achieve here in order to stave off defeat. The advantage of having Laxman as company was reassuring for him.

A well poised match makes a game enthralling and lends exciting drama. Such a circumstance calls upon players to demonstrate their mettle, particularly as adrenaline flows and tension mounts.

What was significant about this match was Tendulkar's presence at a time when India needed him and he did respond graciously, with composure and sound technique. Laxman joined him in an exhibition of rhythmic and composed batting – Laxman, for all his elegant display, was disciplined while Tendulkar was creative in his repertoire of strokes.

The partnership yielded 214 runs of which Tendulkar's innings included 26x4 in 299 balls. Laxman's contribution to the partnership was 68. A hamstring injury denied Tendulkar being part of the ODI which followed.

Once again, Tendulkar and Laxman, reminiscent of their Australian marathon, occupied the crease and built an innings of seven hours, progressing with panache to 176. It was Tendulkar's first century at Kolkata. His dominance and command was outstanding, especially when India needed him. Laxman produced another high century (154), a taste of his legendary 281 vs Australia. They both enjoyed a partnership of 241 in 70 overs. Their efforts dulled West Indian spirit but though 200 in the lead, Ganguly was not interested in a more exciting outcome and allowed the match to peter out into a drawn Test. He was satisfied that India had eventually won the series.

Buoyed by their sparkling all-round performance in the third Test, the West Indies were ignited with complimentary remarks which inspired them to regain pride in their 4-3 defeat of India in the One-Day Internationals.

The Varma-Shuvro report was enthusiastic. "West Indies seemed worthy of a calypso, not a dirge." But the series of defeats was a burden to the West Indies – players, administration and spectating public, were all demoralized. The decision to re-introduce Lara as captain to replace Hooper seemed to gain the approval of the sporting fraternity, particularly as the schedule ahead was demanding. The 2003 schedule included Australia and Sri Lanka in the Caribbean with away from home battles with Zimbabwe and South Africa.

It must be noted that it was Shiv's performances which stood out as they had done in the Caribbean earlier in the year. With such performances he had won the hearts of Indians, even the Indian team.

The Test match averages demonstrate Shiv's performance in comparison with his colleagues:

West Indies – Batting (Test average)

Shiv – 65.00, W. Hinds – 44, C. Gayle – 32, R. Sarwan – 27.6, and C. Hooper – 24.8. The others were single digit averages.

The India press commented on Shiv's diverse assortment of strokes, devoid of reckless flourishes or impetuosity.

India's supremacy over the West Indies was particularly cherished for two reasons – the series victory after 24 years and it was against the reputed calypso cricketers whom the Indians had admired and paid great tribute to since the early years of their cricket relationship.

During his analysis over the years, Hilary Beckles, though willing to give all encouragement and inspiration to the Test team, revealed that the continuing decline wounded his pride and accelerated his loss of faith in West Indies cricket. He did affirm that the West Indies had 'lost its soul' – loss of the enchanted garden of fruitful harvest of its former years. Now it was failure indicating loss of pride, national consciousness, spirit of competitiveness and insensitivity to its glorious historical past. Still, there has always been a sense of optimism in Beckles belief in the West Indian character, and he felt yet hopeful for more fruitful days.

The Bangladesh tour followed soon after. Of the three ODIs West Indies won 2 and 1 drawn. In the two Test series West Indies victory in both matches was no consolation for the West Indian team after this loss to India.

Test 1 Bang	**179**	**W.I**	**397**	**W.I won**
	125			
Test 2 Bang	**267**	**W.I**	**134**	**W.I won**
	54		**191/8**	

Chapter 9

A Historic Victory

In the midst of decline, history is made.

After missing the sub-continent tour versus India and Bangladesh, Lara returned to the fold. With the World Cup of 2003, it was felt that Lara should lead the team. In 2003, he was back at the helm for a second time. He had returned to face the challenges against Australia and Sri Lanka in the Caribbean and subsequently to visit Zimbabwe and South Africa. It was hoped there would be a more mature Lara with the added advantage of his success in his encounters with Australia.

On their visit, the Australian dominated in the first three Tests. Although without Warne for the series and McGrath in the first Test, West Indian encounters were disappointing and dispiriting. The fourth Test was dynamic for the West Indies team and their people. It demonstrated West Indian capabilities when determined and focused on the task at hand. They could achieve the summit of their talent if infused with application. The fourth Test was an inspiration which accelerated their drive to victories against Sri Lanka and Bangladesh but South Africa proved a more challenging opposition.

One of the criticisms levelled against the West Indies was the state of the pitches. Steve Waugh, who had withstood the barrage of West Indies pace and did so courageously, was disappointed in the preparation of the pitches. He expressed the valuable view that West Indian cricket could only develop if their pitches produced fast bowlers. It was a gesture which showed his commitment to competitive cricket which he feared not.

He commented: "I have played 159 Tests," and after his experience in Barbados, "this is the slowest, lowest wicket I have ever played on. All the wickets have been really slow and it's a major problem for cricket in the Caribbean. They're not going to produce any quick bowlers if they keep putting pitches like that."

The series (Test 1-3) turned out to be one of Australian dominance which the West Indies could not counter effectively. Their batting strength is revealed in the statistics – scores of 489, 147 for 1,574 for 4, 273 for 3 and 605 for 9. The Australians proved superior in all aspects of the game. In response there were some reassuring standards of play in West Indian batting - Lara's scores, an encouraging innings of over 50 from Chris Gayle, Ramnaresh Sarwan, D.S. Smith, Marlon Samuels and Shiv's record century at Bourda.

Shiv's phenomenal innings at Bourda (69 ball century) was the third fastest century at that time but has now been relegated to No 5 in line. Wisden (Andrew Ramsey) describes it as a "sublime sideshow to start the series, and an innings of glorious, cavalier defiance." When Shiv came to the wicket, half of his team had been dismissed for 53, but in 108 minutes Shiv proved the calypso spirit was far from dead as he launched himself at fast and slow bowling alike to lift the West Indies to a respectable, if ultimately inadequate 237. He was valiant as he enacted 'wonders with his sword.' The achievement was made the more admirable as his teammates were faltering at 53 for 5 but he presided over the innings progression and seemed to immerse himself in the flow of its movements. Later on as he grew progressively, his stature was enhanced and he continued to traverse the paths of cricket with a singleness of aim. Here he had gained admirable and priceless support from Jacobs.

Test 1 W.I	**237**	**Aus**	**489**	**Aus won**
	398		**147/1**	
Test 2 Aus	**576/4**	**W.I**	**408**	**Aus won**
	238/3		**288**	
Test 3 Aus	**605/9**	**W.I**	**328**	**Aus won**
	8/1		**284**	
Test 4 Aus	**240**	**W.I**	**240**	**W.I won**
	417		**418/7**	

Shiv averaged 42.83 2/100s – 69 ball 100

After the match, Shiv remarked: "When I got to the wicket we were in a difficult situation. What made it a bit comfortable was my home-crowd. The wicket was quite easy paced. I started on a positive note. The first ball went to the boundary. Very often my shots were directed to the boundary, so I got into gear, finding the gaps. The century came up quickly but I did not know it was a 69 - ball century until the announcer on the speaker, Reyaz Hosein, declared it. I felt overjoyed especially as we were not in a good position when I began my innings."

In the first Test, apart from Jacob's 54 when he partnered Shiv, there were no alarming scores and it took one single partnership of 248 from Langer and Ponting to counter the West Indies first innings of 237. A lead of 252 was discouraging for West Indies who in an effort to salvage pride, scored some good innings of 62 by D.S. Smith, 113 from Gayle, 110 from Lara to contribute to 398. But this merely gave Australia a target of 14 which they accomplished with 9 wickets standing.

In the second Test, West Indies were without Lawson, Jacobs and Shiv (a bruised knee). Here Ponting in fine form struck a double hundred (206) with D.S. Lehman (160) in a record third wicket stand of 315 followed by Gilchrist 101. A target of 576/4 was formidable but with Lara's 91 and Gayle's second consecutive century they managed 408. Australia then quickly scored 238/3 to allow West Indies to respond. The only score worthy of mention was Lara's century (122). At the conclusion, Australia were victorious by 118 runs.

Having amassed a mammoth 605, West Indies replies in both innings were inadequate, giving Australia a 9-wicket victory. The margin of victory in all the Tests would discourage any professional team.

It was the popular expectation that a demoralized team would be dejected, dispirited and down-trodden. On the contrary, West Indies performance in the fourth Test in Antigua proved to be a total contrast to the preceding three. However, it was a match smeared by tantrums – Waugh's and Lara's confrontation, and then the McGrath – Sarwan episode – all part of the rough drama in the match.

Both sides had first innings scores of 240, so this left them with a second innings final. Given a 417 target by Australia and enough time to match the score, what was West Indies response? At 164 for 4 with Lara gone after he had played well, West Indies chance looked dismal but the reliable Guyanese pair, Sarwan and Shiv, were a picture of patience and application as they responded to Australia's target. It was a dramatic and suspenseful period in the midst of impending defeat and a crowd with continued hope of success as they built faith in their two heroes. They were clamouring for a burst of brilliance.

A well-crafted partnership between these two stalwarts created a sense of grandeur and immense hope. Sarwan left after a partnership of 123 and a personal score of 105. Shiv, though handicapped, persevered to bring the team close to victory. It further revealed his strength of character and mental fortitude that made others stand in their shoes and wonder at his discipline and courage. He was reaping the harvest of his youthful dreams, unbounded as he responded to his rivals' combative spirit and seemed consumed with unrestrained desire to gain victory. When Sarwan was dismissed, West Indies were 130 behind Australia, Then Jacob went first ball and this revitalised the Australian attack. However, Shiv with his broken finger, applied himself and earned a marvellous century (104) before he was dismissed, leaving 4 wickets to complete this dramatic act. The road to victory was 47 runs and West Indies lower order batsmen brought the match home through their patience and application but not without tension and excitement on the last day.

This was a record chase in Test cricket surpassing the previous record when India in pursuit of 405 gained ascendancy over the West Indies. For the West Indian audience this was celebratory – historic and dramatic. It brought comfort to a people whose hopes had been dashed after the third Test. The partnership delighted and enthralled a cricketing public absorbed in the pursuit of West Indies victory. Patriotic fervour showed its lovely face as there was collective joy when success seemed imminent. Spectator involvement reveals passion that rises out of self-esteem. It was self-esteem for the thousands who awaited and anticipated success. There was hunger for victory on their faces.

When victory was achieved the West Indies audience was ecstatic by this historic feat. In Andrew Ramsey's commentary, he enthused that the "historic win acted as a salve for the wounded pride through the island nations where cricket crazy fans are still struggling to come to terms with their once-mighty team's fall from grace".

The victory was that more rewarding as it was the highest fourth innings run chase. Previously, India had successfully challenged a West Indies target of 405. The spectating public was keen to hear Shiv's thoughts on his innings and partnership with Sarwan. When asked about his role, he recalled: "I broke my finger on the first day, so I didn't field much and just batted. The first innings were even, around 240 each. We needed 418 to win in the second innings and believed that if we batted well enough for long then we would win. The wicket was good. It was about building partnerships and everyone was chipping in. Brian Lara got a few, and then I was batting with Sarwan. I kept saying we needed to keep going and stick with the partnership as long as we could. So we dug in but it was tough out there. Jason Gillespie was running in hard. Brett Lee, too. Glen McGrath was bowling well and Stuart MacGill was hitting the rough outside the left hander's off-stump. I got out early on the final morning, for 104, chasing a wide one, but Vasbert Drakes and Omari Banks kept going and won the game for us. It's still the highest successful Test match run-chase ever."

Handicapped with a broken finger, it was a greet credit to Shiv's achievements as he faced the towering Lee and McGrath. It tells of his courage, steady temperament, skill and discipline to achieve for his team and region – against the best bowling at that time.

With renewed energy and enthusiasm, West Indies boldly confronted Sri Lanka in June 2003 but with the lingering memory of their defeat in 2001. Here, the two Test series concluded with a West Indian victory in the second Test. The first Test was drawn. Shiv would have been a happy man though absent for the tour.

Test 1 SL	**354**	**W.I**	**477/9**	**Match drawn**
	126/0			
Test 2 SL	**208**	**W.I**	**191**	**W.I won**
	194		**212/3**	

With a feeling of optimism, West Indies were steadfast in their resolve to earn victory versus South Africa as this could be cathartic in the context of their humiliating loss in 1998. Their spirit was alive and optimistic but the opposition has always been formidable. But before the greeter challenge with South Africa, West Indies emerged with a 1-0 victory vs Zimbabwe. It was like having practice sessions before the South African encounter.

In the series in Dec 2003/Jan 2004, South African's batting prowess was well-defined in their successful counter to West Indian mediocrity. The pace bowling, lackluster and ineffective batting caused the West Indian to shudder in defeat. It was a 3-0 defeat, another humiliation for the visitors.

Test 1 SA	**561**	**W.I**	**410**	**SA won**
	226/6		**188**	
Test 2 W.I	**264**	**SA**	**658/9**	**SA won**
	329			
Test 3 SA	**532**	**W.I**	**427**	**Match drawn**
	335/3		**354/5**	
Test 4 SA	**604/6**	**W.I**	**301**	**SA won**
	46/0		**348**	

It was agonising to be down-trodden for Lara's team but the consolatory factor was the performances of Shiv, Sarwan and Gayle, coupled with Lara's brilliance on the tour. In the first Test, a formidable target of 561 stared West Indies in the face. As the Test drew to its final stages, West Indies were given a victory target of 378 but an early collapse (3 for 25) proved disconcerting as the demands of the lower order were too onerous. Lara failed in the second innings and Shiv's defiance, though heroic, was not substantial enough to stave off defeat. Then and on other occasions like this, Shiv kindled hope in moments of despair.

South Africa continued to dominate. A second Test innings of 264 was countered by South Africa's 658/9. A target of 394, though challenged, was not surpassed. There was resistance from Sarwan (114) and also Shiv's brilliant innings of 109. Though hampered by injury, he masterly stroked 81 of his 109 in boundaries. In the midst of defeat, it was a brilliant light in the darkness. Though bravely challenged, West Indies suffered a loss by an innings and 65 runs.

Their attempts to repair the ruins of the first two Tests by mounting challenges in Test 3 and Test 4 were unsuccessful. Faced with fiery pace, though not victorious, their batting showed sparks of brilliance.

The team departed, wounded and dejected. It was a series where the hosts had held the advantage and stamped their presence in all aspects of the game. In contrast, West Indian bowling showed its inadequacies. The bowlers seemed incapable of capturing 20 wickets in a match. With such wounds the team returned home, reflecting on methods of recovery and constructing anew if they were to withstand the rigours of international cricket.

Chapter 10

A Fragile, Splintered Team

A proof of West Indies descent into a vortex of despondency and failure

Hugh Chevallier

After their defeat in South Africa, the team journeyed to the Caribbean with the prospect of a contest with England at home. Critics were vitriolic in condemnation, describing them as a "fragile, splintered team". Not only was the team in anguish but also the Caribbean audience felt wounded and disillusioned after the team's pathetic display vs South Africa. However, there was hope of recovery with the consolation of playing at home.

Sabina Park was host to the first encounter in March 2004, and this started on a positive note as both teams were close in first innings scores. Subjected to fiery pace from the English bowlers, the West Indian batsmen rallied to 311. It was a promising start where pace was dominant.

Test 1 W.I	**311**	**Eng**	**339**	**Eng won**
	47		**20/0**	
Test 2 W.I	**208**	**Eng**	**319**	**Eng won**
	209		**99/3**	
Test 3 W.I	**224**	**Eng**	**226**	**Eng won**

	94		**93/2**	
Test 4 W.I	**604/6**	**Eng**	**285**	**Match drawn**
	781./5		**422/5**	

Brian Lara 400 not out regains record with 400 runs eclipsing Matthew Hayden's 380.

When the English batted they were also subjected to fiery pace bowling but managed to outdo the West Indies by 28 runs. It was almost even at the end of the first innings, but a dramatic collapse in the West Indian second innings was disconcerting and painful as the team was trounced, culminating in their lowest total of 47 runs. A ruthless spell of accurate bowling by Steve Harmison dictated the outcome with his spell of 12 –3 – 8 – 7 (seven wickets for eight runs).

In an appraisal of Harmison's career, John Stern, remarked that it was a 'quantum leap - - - bowling - - - but asking a question of batsmen every single ball".

It seemed to many English cognoscenti and aficionados that this was a strong response to West Indies' humiliation of England in 1998, a response for the decimation England endured with a score of 46 runs. Then, it was Ambrose and now, it was Harmison.

After their first victory, England went on to capture the second Test by 7 wickets at the Queen's Park Oval in Trinidad. This was followed by another victory in the third Test at Kensington Oval, Barbados. It was a period of embarrassment for West Indian batsmen who failed to counter the audacious spells of pace bowling. Here in Cozier's commentary, it was a demoralized team collapsing on an animated pitch. In the third Test, there was another West Indian failure in which they were dismissed for 94.

The senior players were disappointing. In the first Test, Sarwan made a pair, Gayle 5 and 19, Lara 23 and 0 and Shiv 7 and 0. In this Test series, except for a few creditable innings in the ODI's, Shiv seemed "out of sorts". So oft it happens in one's endeavours – inability to sustain a high degree of performance. There was much reflection on the loss. There were critical reviews on the state of West Indian cricket, the lack of awareness of their historical past and the need for emotional inspiration to improve performance, focusing on their role with commitment.

Lara was maligned for the failures and it was felt that the players' skills were not being fully exploited. The Press was punishing in their critical comments on Lara and insistent that he had to repair the ruins.

Amidst the criticism, West Indies entered the last Test with the hope of salvaging some pride on a ground known for the team's positive performance.

The series concluded with a 3-0 England victory. The last encounter in Antigua was a drawn Test. Here was a milestone - an epic event which brought life to the West Indian public, revealing the rich possibilities of the game. Six months before this Test, Matthew Hayden had eclipsed Lara's record when he accumulated 380 against Zimbabwe. Here, Lara surpassed Hayden with a score of 400 not out against the dominant English team, enhancing his personal glory and collective West Indian spirit, pride and image.

The West Indies dominated this Test with a score of 751 for 5 but was followed by a match saving effort in the second English innings. Though it was a magnificent individual performance there were still dark clouds over West Indian cricket. Lara lamented the fate of his troops but hoped that his performance would help to foster greater cohesion among the islands.

It was a match that Shiv had not played but he so wished he had been there to accompany Lara once again.

While the accolades streamed in on Lara's epic performance and the spectacle that accompanied it, the main preoccupation dwelt on the West Indian return visit to England for the Test series in Jul/August 2004. It was soon after the English tour of the Caribbean.

The onerous responsibility of attending to a team, lacking in purpose, and a seeming inability to hone talents, whose interest was directed to commercialism which began to infect the sport, was indeed a challenge. Captains before Lara were experiencing the same traumas of defeat and fluctuating performances. Richardson suffered frustrating periods, Hooper, Walsh, Adams and Lara all inherited fledgling talents, inconsistent in their performances. Sarwan showed promise, as did Gayle but Shiv held his own on many occasions. Beckles asserted that the players were not part of the historical and cultural tradition from which they had emerged; they were oblivious to the progressive transformation of cricketing teams which they encountered.

The tour to England was another calamitous story. England had nurtured a young, fresh team full of purpose and enthusiasm and were also aware of West Indian mediocrity which they had hoped to exploit during the tour. They saw no true indication of West Indian emergence as competitors. To them, that was a glory of the past. For England, it was a time of reprisal for the frustration they had been subjected to in the 70s – 80s. They were inspired by their victory in the Caribbean earlier in the year and were prepared to never let down their guard. They were resolute in their quest for supremacy.

In the first Test at Lords, Lara opted to field though he had won the toss. It was his belief that his paceman could exploit the overcast conditions but they proved ineffective. With the failed efforts from the bowlers and the change in climate, England began to flourish. A score of 568 was a daunting task for their opponents. In response, West Indies opening partnership of 118 looked encouraging but they were able to accumulate only 416. A deficit of 152 did not augur well towards the final outcome. It was only Shiv's stay of 10 hours for an unbeaten 128 that challenged the English attack. Shiv continued his good form in the second innings with an unbeaten 97. His innings seemed flushed with a flicker of light but he was denied the second century though unbeaten in both innings. It was a well-deserved record he had missed.

Wisden noted that "Chanderpaul, back to his crustacean best after an indifferent run, nudged and nurdled and unfurled the occasional bent-kneed belt through the covers – to his 11th century". Shiv had partnered Dwayne Bravo for a decent stand and then with Jacobs and Banks they avoided the follow-on.

In the second innings, West Indian response was dampened when D.S. Smith and Sarwan were early dismissals. Gayle was aggressive with a score of 81 and Lara was bowled for 44. Only Shiv remained the immovable object. He was subjected to physical pain in his arm and knee but persevered to 97 not out, just 3 short of a record twin centuries. He remained at the wicket to the end (10 hours and 14 minutes), a lesson in application, endurance and skill.

This innings revealed a man with a singleness of purpose, addicted to the code of infinite involvement in his mission – a unique, phenomenal revelation of man's perseverance. It was discomfiting that Shiv could not have achieved the memorable, distinctive feat of a century in each innings. Any performer with such an outstanding record in that Test would be either agonizing or in a dejected state of mind but Shiv stoically endured the disappointment of such denial.

The advantage gained in the first innings took its toll on the West Indies. With a deficit of 152 and a second innings 267, the response to England's target was not significant. Lara's 11 and 44 were inconsequential towards West Indian recovery.

In the following Test at Birmingham, England retained the Wisden Trophy with a victory by 256 runs within four days. Again England's handsome 561 dictated the progress of the match. Here it was only Shiv and Sarwan who challenged the target but were in a large deficit. A follow-on decision was not entertained by captain Vaughn, and Lara's 95 and Sarwan's 139 efforts were of no consequence in the final outcome. Faced with a target of 478, West Indies gathered

222, thus succumbing by 256 runs. During the match the only vestige of joy was Lara's achievement of his 10,000 runs.

The critics ensured that the West Indies were crushed in their verbal onslaught. After the second loss at Edgbaston, Hugh Chevallier in an incisive burst deemed the four-day loss as significant. For him it was "a proof of the West Indies descent into a vortex of despondency and failure." He saw West Indies in its gloom and nadir with Lara on the field experiencing "just lonely, anguished suffering".

The third Test at Manchester, began on quite a positive note for the West Indies with a score of 395 and a contained England at 40 for 3 but they were not able to capitalize on this and in the process, England mustered 330, only 65 short of the West Indian total. The West Indian second innings was suicidal. They were dismissed for 165 (lowest score on that tour) leaving England to challenge 230. Here it was a 7-wicket victory for England and a mark of their supremacy.

A whitewash was the utter misery that brought the tour to a gloomy end. Responding to a total of 470 at the Oval, a 152- West Indian response was pathetic. Lara's effort of 79 was inconsequential to the outcome. However, they did offset the 318 lead with a 318 total, leaving England one run for victory.

The series revealed once again West Indies' fragility and decline; it was a sad, unpleasant time for Caribbean cricket. Lara's efforts were not supported by his colleagues except for Gayle and Shiv, but these were not substantial enough to challenge England's dominance.

Test 1 Eng	**568**	**W.I**	**416**	**Eng won**
	325/5		**267**	
Test 2 Eng	**566/9**	**W.I**	**336**	**Eng won**
	248		**222**	
Test 3 W.I	**395/9**	**Eng**	**330**	**Eng won**
	165		**231/3**	
Test 4 Eng	**470**	**W.I**	**152**	**Eng won**
	4/0		**318**	

West Indies Man of the Series – Shiv Chanderpaul

Shiv averaged 72.83 (1st placed) 1/100 2/50s

The tour revealed the ineptitude and inertia which had begun to characterise the quality of West Indies performance. The batting performances while showing some sparks of brilliance, were seldom shaped into solid responses to defy the English bowlers. Shiv, according to Wisden, was 'resolute as ever' but also succumbed to England's persistence. He did emerge West Indies' Man of the Series. In both West Indian Test Batting Averages and Tour Averages (other first class matches) he stood at the top. In the Tests: an aggregate of 457, 128 highest score in the series and an average of 72.83; in the overall average – 583 runs at 64.77. The only other batsman to surpass an average of 50 in both formats (Test and Tour) was Gayle with averages of 50 and 51.72. It was another catastrophic conclusion for West Indies cricket and a lesson, that all hoped, the players would learn from this disastrous tour. It was sad to read Fazeer Mohammed's comment that "England administered a three-day whipping of West Indies that sealed a clean sweep of the series and emphasized the staggeringly swift decline of the Caribbean side from supremely professional invincibles to a temperamental, undisciplined rabble".

Still, some measure of relief from the discomfort was welcomed after their capture of the Champions Trophy against England in the final encounter. The victories over Pakistan and South Africa gave them a berth in the finals vs England. In response to 217, the match gained intensity when Shiv was dismissed in pursuit of the target. With the score 147 for 8, the lower order players, Bradshaw and Browne, held their own and steadily steered the West Indies to victory. To accomplish and be the recipient of this global trophy was a moral boost for West Indian cricket.

Anand Varsu who reported on the match was enthused by the West Indian victory. The performances, he described, as one "that shone like a beacon through the darkness". And Wisden describes the West Indian feat "as soul-stirring – a relief to the West Indies, an anodyne not only for the losses suffered but for the natural disasters which devastated the Caribbean. Their triumph brought ecstasy and joy of relief after the annihilation suffered earlier in the year. If this euphoric moment was short-lived, its colour and vitality made it memorable".

This was the first victory for many years and while it was lauded by many, there were those who were realistic in assessing the state of West Indian cricket. While Dilip Premachandran recalled the great feats of West Indian cricket, he added the rational thought that “few would delude themselves into thinking that one glorious evening in the Oval sunlight was the harbinger of another era of unprecedented success. Those days had vanished, never to return”.

However, in the first quarter of 2021 some spark of resurgence had surfaced in the Test contest with Bangladesh. It was hoped that this positive start would continue as the year progressed. It was also hoped that the West Indian team could prove Premachandran wrong.

Chapter 11

Shiv At The Helm

The drought seemed to have no end.

West Indies decline at the turn of the century manifested itself not only in cricket performance but in the team's mentality. Here was a fragmented, fractured and discordant group of players. It was a dispirited lot that brought agony to the West Indian community. Turbulence reigned, more so as there was continuing conflict with the West Indian Cricket Board. Team sponsorship became an issue and this further aggravated the team's morale.

Wisden reports on the problematic issue:

The long-time sponsors of the international team, Cable & Wireless, weary of association with failure, had made way for Digicel, their rivals in the world of Caribbean telecoms. The trouble was that six leading players – vice-captain Ramnaresh Sarwan, Dwayne Bravo, Fidel Edwards, Chris Gayle, Ravi Rampaul and Dwayne Smith – retained personal contracts with Cable and Wireless, a situation the West Indies Board said ruled them out of the Test selection. The Players' Association took issue with this, and civil war broke out. Although West Indies captain Brian Lara was not directly affected, he chose to side with the six, stating that if they were considered ineligible, he was too. Some sort of temporary truce was eventually brokered when the players terminated their personal contracts but not in time to prevent a weakened side, under new captain,

Shivnarine Chanderpaul, taking the field in the first Test. And it was far from a lasting peace, as became clear when the West Indies Board struggled to raise a team to tour Sri Lanka in July.

The South African visit of early April – May 2005 proved onerous for West Indian cricket. The South Africans, realizing West Indies problems and their struggles, came in a positive mood to the Caribbean. The new leader – Chanderpaul – at the helm had proven his skills as a batsman but he had the experience as a captain at territorial level, in his country of Guyana. He was positioned as leader in a time of declining fortunes and constant feuding between Board and players. This made his role even more demanding. He was now presiding over a fledging team. Everyone looked towards his performance, one which diverged from the accustomed role of batsman to the expanded player/ leader role at Test level. This responsibility was thrust on him and the challenge was more onerous with a fledging group. The team included only one survivor from the last test – i.e. Shiv Chanderpaul. It was bereft of experienced players, 'short of class and collective wisdom'. The loss of Lara and six other teammates due to their contractual disputes was no consolation. It only spelt gloom.

Test 1 W.I	**543/5**	**SA**	**188**	**Match drawn**
			269/4	
Test 2 W,I	**347**	**SA**	**398**	**SA won**
	194		**146/2**	

Test 3 W.I	**296**	**SA**	**548/9**	**SA won**
	166			
Test 4 SA	**588/6**	**W.I**	**747**	**Match drawn**
	127/1			

Shiv averaged 90.00 – (1st placed) 2/100s 1/50

In the series the drought of failures continued and there was further frustration through a lack of direction in West Indian cricket. In the four-Test contest, South Africa emerged victorious leading 2-0 with a drawn two Tests. South Africa continued to dominate with five victories in the One-Day Internationals.

The first Test was astonishing to both enthusiasts and sceptics who stood in awe as the match took its course. The team had, surprisingly to all, displayed a batting performance which could have earned them victory but South Africa's resolve and grit denied them.

It is significant to relate the events or the course of that first Test in light of the final outcome. It was a dramatic start to a Test match, the sequence of which, took the sails out of a West Indian victory. The prolific innings of Wavell Hinds (213) and Shiv Chanderpaul (203) established a formidable position for the West Indies. This run-feast seemed to blunt the South Africans who managed only a 188 in response. However, the follow-on response showed a resolute South Africa with the sustained efforts of Jacques Kallis and Hershelle Gibbs in denying a West

Indian victory. With a sense of stoicism, the South Africans held their ground; it was a mature and methodical approach, one of discipline and application to the challenge at hand. Their stoicism as evident between lunch and tea of the last day when they added 45 in 30 overs is a testament to their unwavering resolve.

Shiv's comment revealed some measure of satisfaction with their efforts. He pointed out: "We came in as underdogs; we scored more than 500 runs and our bowlers did well. I don't think we would want to change much about this match." Deep down he felt victory had eluded him but his small consolation was his Man-of-the-Match award.

The second Test saw the return of Lara after the debacle with the Board appeared to have been resolved. The re-instatement of the key players through this 'temporary truce' now added strength and experience to the team. It was Lara's turn to be skippered by his colleague, Shiv. Though Lara's brilliance shone through his versatility of strokeplay, Makhaya Ntini's bowling skills decimated the batting line-up. Lara's supreme mastery brought him his 27th Test century from 113 Tests. He was placed third in a list of highest run-scorers by an individual batsman, placing him behind Allan Border and Steve Waugh. The West Indian total of 347 mounted through Lara's 196 with the support of Gayle 32 and Shiv 35. South Africa could not be undone as they led by 51 runs. Another West Indian batting failure in the second innings, with only Sarwan's 107, provided little comfort as South Africa countered effectively.

South Africa sealed victory in the series in the third Test

match. A West Indian 296 in the first innings was countered by a robust 548 for 9. The West Indies then crumbled for 166 giving South Africa a wide margin of an innings and 86 runs.

Here again, Lara flourished and secured a splendid 176 and it was Shiv who bravely responded with 53 runs to his credit.

In the second innings it was only Shiv who resisted with 31 runs as he tried to combat the South African bowling.

The team's performance was atrocious and the bowling lacked Test quality. Faced with a deficit of 252, the collapse of front-line batsmen augured disaster for the team. Persistence came from Chanderpaul's 31 but it was not sustained, neither was their support.

Antigua's fourth Test venue again produced mammoth totals on both sides. In each there were four centuries. Among the West Indies was the massive 311 by Gayle who together with the other centurions enjoyed the featherbed wicket. Performances here were now becoming inconsequential as the wickets offered no challenge on many occasions.

With humiliating defeats, West Indies continued to flounder. Both players and public suffered the pangs of defeat. This resulted in the public's growing lack of interest in the team's efforts and disillusionment surfaced.

In the following encounter with Pakistan in May/June 2005, West Indies suffered a 3-0 ODI defeat. The disenchantment of the spectating public was evident in the low attendances at Barbados and Jamaica. In the crucial two-

Test series, the West Indies were triumphant in the first with a margin of 276 but then succumbed to Pakistan by 136 in the second encounter. In the first Test, Shiv determined as always, produced two remarkable innings of 92 and 153. Again the century in each innings eluded him. It was not without Lara's prolific scoring with an entertaining 130 and 48. Lara's and Shiv's efforts combined with Fidel Edwards' burst of pace ensured a West Indies victory. Pakistan was dismissed for 144 but Shiv declined the follow-on option with a lead of 201. In the second innings, he extended the lead with a score of 371, thus challenging Pakistan to pursue 573 for victory. It was a challenge beyond them and Shiv's team secured a victory – the first for Chanderpaul as captain. He was also awarded Man of the Match.

Test 1 W.I	**345**	**Pak**	**144**	**W.I won**
	371		**296**	
Test 2 Pak	**374**	**W.I**	**404**	**Pak won**
	309		**143**	

1st Test – Shiv, Man of the Match

Pakistan, never to be underestimated, responded with alacrity in the second Test. A 'perplexing failure' with the bat in the West Indies second innings caused their defeat. A target of 280 for victory proved futile as Pakistan's bowling armoury reduced West Indies efforts to disastrous failure. A 1-1 result was West Indies sole consolation.

Amidst the ruins of the once 'great house', further problems surfaced as the visit to Sri Lanka was scheduled in July 2005. The struggling parties, the West Indies Cricket Board and the Players' Association debated over sponsorship and this resulted in the withdrawal of the original group of players. Lara, Gayle and Sarwan were part of this impasse. As a result, a relatively new team had to be selected to visit Sri Lanka.

Test 1 W.I	**285**	**SL**	**227**	**SL won**
	113		**172/4**	
Test 2 SL	**150**	**W.I**	**148**	**SL won**
	375/7		**137**	

Against this background of controversy and unease, it was not surprising that defeat stared them in the face. It was only Shiv, in his 86th Test match and with 14 centuries to his credit, who had the experience to counter the Sri Lankan attack. The newly-formed team showed a fair measure of resistance and were no less competent than the 2007 team which had suffered a cruel defeat. However, despite their efforts, the team succumbed to the swing of Vaas and the spin of Muttiah Muralitharan. And with the numerous goings-on in West Indian cricket, there was a loss of faith and a sense of frustration occasioned by both the controversies and repeated failures. However, the impasse was resolved as best as possible and a full team including the more experienced players journeyed to Australia for another contest.

This new series was also depressing in its further revelation of sterility. Continuing mediocrity and lack of passion had been evident since the turn of the new millennium. It seemed as if a loss of faith and confidence in their performance detracted from any positive aspiration they might have harboured. Also evident was that lack of true introspection and deep desire to elevate their stature which Lara had alluded to in his discourse on the reasons for West Indian failures. The Australian tour made no significant difference to performance and the West Indians floundered to defeats by 379 runs, nine and seven wicket defeats as the Tests progressed to their anticipated conclusion. One of the consequences of decline was the lack of admiration for the team by its native supporters and foreign counterparts. Any show of support was sparse but the damning effect of decline was the curtailed length of tours. West Indies tours had been reduced from five Test series to three because of the growing lack of interest in the West Indies now notorious fallibility and lack of challenge.

The unchallenging cricket, Shiv explained, was due to the consequence of a disunited bunch of unruly players who were deliberately subverting his leadership.

Shiv commented: “They seemed not interested in playing under my captaincy. In Australia it was quite noticeable as umpire Rudy Kursten approached me and spoke about the players’ attitude. Kursten was so disturbed that he spoke to coach, Bennett King, telling him about the players’ behaviour on the field.

One of the problems was the setting of the field. Some players would not listen to me; I would put a player on the boundary line and he would stay clear off the boundary and move when he wished. The problem became more serious when the pacemen were bowling at a slow over rate. It meant that I would be penalized for slow over rate. I had to counter this by bringing on the spinners to speed up the over rate. This was a problem we had in Australia.

I remember in a match, Guyana vs Jamaica, when Chris Gayle was aggressive, hitting the ball one bounce to the boundary. I had to put a fielder at backward point and in no time we got Gayle. But Colin Croft in the commentary box was saying it was the worst fielding placing he had seen in his career. I know what I was doing. And that position is used presently many times.

I had been captain of Guyana's team for ten years and I know about captaincy. When I was asked to lead the team, I remember talking to my manager Chris Thackoor Persaud and Mr. Eddy Luckoo who did not hesitate to advise me to take up the challenge.

I also recall after my award form UWI St Augustine, Colin Croft saw me in a plane flight and ignored me. Is this how we are going to unite as a West Indian people and as a team? Even Richardson, Walsh and Adams had problems with the players. With this opposition I began to reconsider my role as captain."

Test 1 Aus	**435**	**W.I**	**210**	**Aus won**
	283/2		**129**	
Test 2 W.I	**149**	**W.I**	**406**	**Aus won**
	334		**78/1**	
Test 3 W.I	**405**	**Aus**	**428**	**Aus won**
	204		**82/3**	

A "ruthless victory" is Peter English's description of the first Test encounter between Australia and the West Indies on Australian soil. This Test brought Australia's victory to 46 versus the West Indies; they had also suffered 32 defeats in 100 Test matches. In a show of bravery and daring, Shiv, offered the Australians the opportunity to start the innings. It seemed to work successfully and the Australians were struggling at 111 for 4 but once again West Indies faltered as Ponting took the initiative with a century and this was bolstered by lower order batting success. West Indies exploited the early advantage but then faltered. Fazeer Mohammed's critical comment on their performances is most appropriate: "But more often than not it is that nagging inconsistency, that almost chronic inability to withstand prolonged periods of sustained pressure from the opposition that forces them, as it were, to capitulate with disastrous consequences". Against a target of 435, a paltry 210 was the response. An unfortunate decision against Lara curtailed his innings to 30. This call had made a difference with Lara in prolific form. A target of 509 at the concluding stage of the match was insurmountable as West Indies faltered to 129. A demoralized team continued to be hurt by the competitive spirit of the opposing side.

Defeat and failure continued to plague the team which could only muster 149 in the first innings of the second Test. Australia's 406 was too onerous for a successful West Indies response. Here again Lara was unfortunate to be dismissed in a poor caught out decision. His personal score was 45 but on 12 he had surpassed Steve Waugh's 10,927 (the second highest individual Test score). The final Test proved to be another dispiriting blow for West Indies but their consolation was Lara's ascending to the highest individual Test score of 11,174 runs having surpassed Border's record. His score in this Test was a monumental 226.

An embattled, weary team with weaknesses exposed had shown no signs of resurgence. The critics were ruthless in their indignation and were utterly incensed as the West Indies continued to suffer failures. The dismal displays which followed in the New Year of Feb/Mar 2006 vs New Zealand gave further justification for mounting cynicism among cricketing journalists. The New Zealand Press was audacious in their mockery of West Indies' performance. It was a tirade that was embarrassing to both players and the West Indian public. In the One Day encounters West Indies surrendered 1-4, were defeated in the 20-20 match and again summarily beaten in two matches of the three Test contest. They drew one.

Test 1 NZ	**275**	**W.I**	**257**	**NZ won**
	272		**263**	
Test 2 W.I	**192**	**NZ**	**372**	**NZ won**
	215		**37/0**	
Test 3	**Rain**	**W.I**	**256/4**	

Earlier on, during the defeat against Pakistan, Fazeer Mohammed, though critical of West Indies match failures and technical difficulties, made the generous comment that they were "one of the best batting line-ups in the world". He gave credit to their performances vs Australia (the 418 victory), 751 vs England, and 474 vs South Africa. But it must be noted that these occasions, though commendable, were rare. The passion to contest with vigour, courage and a sense of patriotism was absent as evidenced in their numerous encounters dating from the late 1900s to the early years of the new century.

As West Indies' cricket decline became more obvious, so did the criticisms intensify. Commentary in different forms described the frailties and disastrous performances of the team. Both critics at home and abroad did not fail in their ruthless assessment. During the New Zealand tour, West Indian performances were highlighted in the media, sending a chill through West Indian supporters. The New Zealand Press tirade angered Lara who responded in defence of West Indian tradition, performance and dominance over the many years. It was blatantly unfair, in Lara's view, to be subjected to such media ridicule.

Shiv felt it was in his interest and the region's, to resign, as it was the opportune time to abdicate leadership in order to concentrate on his batting. The role as batsman in the team was of greater significance for all. And with such determination, his batting over the years was courageous and impressive. Later he had been highly successful in his career, gaining his place among Wisden cricketers of the year in 2007 and in Wisden World Class Test XI. In Price Waterhouse's ranking he had the honour of being No. 1 Batsman in the world.

Shiv's resignation made way for a new captain.

In his assessment of West Indies cricket performances at the turn of the century Rohan Kanhai had noted Shiv's potential and progress as a batsman and felt that players with such potential needed guidance. He therefore referred

Shiv to Chris Thachorpersaud in Orlando. This marked a turning point in Shiv's career as he was on the right path through Chris' intervention. Shiv continued to progress with an almost incredible degree of success. With West Indian failure during his reign, in consultation with Chris, he gave up the captaincy to concentrate on his batting and he then demonstrated to the cricketing world his ability as a batsman.

Chapter 12

Lara Back At The Helm

The defeat by New Zealand in February/March 2006 hastened Shiv's resignation. The two Test series in Don Cameron's reports, was described "as an unsatisfactory tour, featuring a West Indies team that did not know how to win and a New Zealand one flattered by the scoreline." Shiv's average was the lowest in his career – 14.80 – a significant blow to his reputation and self-esteem.

On their return home, the Zimbabweans with a fledgling team waited for a seven-match One Day Series (replacing two Tests, 5 ODIs due to the Zimbabwe Cricket Board's decision to suspend Test Cricket competition for a brief period. A bitter feud between Zimbabwe players and Board Officials resulted in a change of the schedule. Once again, for the third time, Lara resumed captaincy. In this series, Shiv's form re-ignited with his achievement as Man of the Series with scores of 46, 93, 51 and 45 in the matches he played.

The Indian expedition to the Caribbean in May-June 2006 was adjudged critically. Some expressed enthusiasm with West Indies' performance though they lost the Test series. There were those who were unimpressed by both teams. Indian sportswriter, Siddhartha Vaidyananthan described it as "high on expectation but how low on productivity." In the One-Day International series, West Indies dominated 4-1, much to the consternation of the Indians. They were astonished by such defeat after a considerable run of ODI victories.

Sunil Gavaskar, who was on tour with a Television commentary team saw it as a well-deserved West Indies victory and a well-deserved Indian loss. But later in the series, delight pervaded the Indian camp as it had become their first series win in the Caribbean since Gavaskar's triumphant maiden series of 1971.

The One-Day series saw West Indies gaining the ascendancy after a first match loss. They ended with a 4-1 margin of victory. Shiv did not prosper in the ODI's but he managed second spot in the Test Averages. His scores of 24, 62, 30, 54, 97 n.o and 11, 10 and 13 gave him an average of 43 behind Daren Ganga's 49.14. Ganga had topped the average and scored one century and one innings over 50 and emerged Man of the Match. The low averages of Lara's 26.37, Gayle's 34.37 and Sarwan's 32.12 justify Vaidyananthan's critical comment on the low level of productivity.

The Test series saw fluctuations in fortunes at the very outset. At St. John's, Antigua, a paltry 241 in India's first innings was met with a healthy West Indies response of 371, thus gaining a lead of 130. This augured well for West Indian cricket success in light of the 4-1 dramatic ODIs achievement, but with great resilience and courage, India fought back to a memorable 521. It was a dramatic twist as the West Indies were given a 391 target for victory.

Test 1 India	**241**	**W.I**	**371**	**Match drawn**

	521/6		**298/9**	
Test 2 India	**588/8**	**W.I**	**215**	**Match drawn**
			294/7	
Test 3 W.I	**581**	**India**	**362**	**Match drawn**
	172/6		**298/4**	
Test 4 India	**200**	**W.I**	**103**	**India won**
	171		**219**	

Shiv averaged 43.00 (2nd placed)

Early wickets fell – Sarwan (1) and Lara (0) were early departures but with Daren Ganga's dismissal on 36, Gayle and Shiv consolidated in an effort to stave off defeat. India's first onslaught included Gayle's wicket for a well-deserved 60. Shiv played with greater fluency, 'timing exquisitely through the covers and striking majestically to the boundary' but at 62, he fell victim to Anil Kumble's, caught out at slip for a ball which touched the pad. An erroneous umpiring decision ended his defiant response.

He would have made a significant difference had he not been unfortunately dismissed. In such an enterprising mood, he was capable of a century and would have at least avoided having to struggle to save the match.

The lower order struggled in facing the challenge. To the very end there was tension. Collymore survived a last ball lbw appeal with the score 298 for 9 – a narrow escape for the West Indies. It was an opportunity lost for India, the match being remembered for Shiv's resolute effort and determination to save his side the ignominy of defeat, particularly so as the West Indies were dominant at the outset of this match.

The second Test at the Gros Islet, St. Lucia (Beausejour Ground) was comforting to the Indians who amassed a mammoth 588 for 8 declared – a total to distress any opposing team. A West Indian response of 215 gave India the chance to secure victory by an innings but rain intervened.

West Indies' response, however, at first threatened India's optimism. Lara scored 120, his 32rd Test century. His departure left the lower order to contend with India's thrust to victory. Once again, Shiv, with the support of Dwayne Bravo frustrated the Indians. The battle those two waged against the Indians – Shiv (54) and Bravo (47) would have certainly pleased their captain.

St. Kitts was the venue for the third Test. An impressive West Indian score of 581 presented a serious challenge to their rivals. Though Lara failed, the rest of the batting did not disappoint. Gayle's 83. Darren Ganga's 135, Sarwan's 116, Samuel's 87 and Shiv's 97 not out created a formidable platform for a West Indian offensive. Wisden reports that Shiv was left stranded at 97. Shiv recalls: "Harbajan Singh had taken a hat-trick and there was no one to partner me towards a century."

India replied with 362 and this gave the West Indies a lead of 219. In the driver's seat, the West Indies concluded a second innings giving India a 391 target in 88 overs. It was a total that could make India think of winning. India responded with great enterprise. With a fine display of batsmanship from Jaffer (54), Sehwag 65, VVS Laxman 63, Dravid 68 not out, Yuvray on 8 not out, India were not too far from having a chance to win but were 93 short of victory at the end. Yet to deliver were Kaif, Kumble and Harbhajan, all capable with the bat. Wisden reports that "West Indies moved guards into position, and defended the vaults" A drawn Test was the outcome.

In a bowlers' dominated match at Sabina Park, Jamaica in the fourth Test, India achieved a 49 run victory. It was an intensely fought contest with low scores – India 200 as against West Indies 103 in the first innings. In the second innings with another paltry 171 total, the challenge to West Indies was a 286 run target. In both innings India's spin attack brought victory to the team. In the second innings it was Anil Kumble who led the forces capturing six wickets. The West Indies fell short of the target by 49 runs. The victory seemed slim but it bought the series win for India. Apart for scores Lara's 26, Sarwan's 51, Ramdin's 62 and Bravo's 33, every other batsman, including the reliable Shiv, failed.

In a series which was described as one of low productivity, five of India's batsmen attained the statistical average of 58.1 plus. In the West Indian camp only two batsmen had respectable averages – Daren Ganga 49.14 and Shivnarine Chanderpaul 43.00. The productivity level was certainly low for the West Indies.

Fluctuating performances marked West Indian cricket from the late nineties onwards but it was fluctuation which was more on the downside with some periods of glimmer and hope.

The West Indian team embarked upon an extended tour to the Far-East to participate in tournaments which included One-Dayers in Malaysia and India. These encounters in both countries were expressive of West Indies' skills in One-Day rivalries.

Shiv remembers: "We were doing very well but on our way to India we were afflicted with diahorrea. It was horrible when we had to enter people's homes to empty our bowels. The food poisoning took a toll on us. At one point, Chris Gayle and I were on drips to improve our health. Some thought the food was deliberately spiked."

After their sojourn in both countries, they visited Pakistan in Nov of 2006. The itinerary included three Tests and five ODIs. From their display on the field it was strikingly apparent that their lacklustre performances were due to physical exhaustion.

Craig Cozier reports:-

"It was a disappointing end to a long tour for West Indies who had started by reaching the finals of a One-day tournament in Malaysia, and the champion Trophy in India."

Lara was outstanding with 122 in the first Test at Lahore and then a blistering 216 in the second at Multan. In this second Test at Multan, his first 100 came off 77 balls – his fastest century.

Test 1 W.I	**206**	**Pak**	**485**	**Pak won**
	291		**13/1**	
Test 2 Pak	**357**	**Pak**	**591**	**Match drawn**
	461/7			
Test 3 Pak	**304**	**W.I**	**260**	**Pak won**
	399/6		**244**	

Shiv averaged 41.00 (2nd placed)

In the first Test, West Indies' modest 206 met a solid reply of 485 with a remarkable 192 from Mohammad Yousuf who would continue to be the thorn in West Indies side during this series. In response to Pakistan's forcefulness, Lara and Shiv produced a fourth day fightback in a stand of 137. But neither his 122 and Shiv's 81 could stop Pakistan. After Lara's and Shiv's dismissals, the lower order crumbled, thus giving Pakistan the lead in the series.

The second Test was drawn in a high scoring match. Pakistan achieved 357 and 461, set against West Indies 591. A West Indies thrust to win was deterred by 'faulty catching' and Pakistan survived to earn a draw.

The third Test belonged to Pakistan with Mohammad Yousuf's centuries in both innings. Yousuf scored 102 and 124 in these two innings and made Pakistan's position impregnable. Through efforts from Ganga (81), Gayle (40), Ramdin (50) and Shiv in the first innings, West Indies struggled to come to terms with Pakistan's score. A determined 81 from Ganga in the first innings and Ramdin's 50 gave West Indies some hope but to no avail as the team score of 260 could not match the Pakistan total. Set a target of 440 for victory, West Indies faltered. In a last attempt to produce a remarkable score, Shiv's 69 was the only silver lining but not enough to gain victory or deny defeat. Pakistan took the series 2-0.

In the One-Day International matches, Shiv played in two matches due to the after effects of discomfort suffered when he left Malaysia. In the fourth match his score of 60 and Samuel's 100 set their team on a victory path. In the fifth match, his score of 101 did not help them to claim victory.

It is interesting to note that the Test averages revealed Lara at 89.6 average with an aggregate of 448 runs and Shiv's 205 averaged 41.00. No other batsman went beyond 40, a disastrous statistical batting failure. It was a period of cricket that brought no joy to the public and even greater dispondency to the team. Though they had flourished well in their attempt at the Champion Trophy in India. It was very obvious that the West Indies players were tired and dispirited during their last encounters.

Left: Shivnarine Chanderpaul (C) plays a shot watched by Australian wicketkeeper Adam Gilchrist during the second cricket Test in Hobart, 17 November 2005. Chanderpaul was eventually out on 39 with the West Indies 124 for 5 at tea.

Above: Shiv kisses the ground after reaching his century WI vs South Africa 2003.

Above: Shivnarine Chanderpaul looks back at his stumps after playing Australian fast bowler Glenn McGrath onto his wickets in the first test at the Gabba in Brisbane 26 November. The West Indians lost the first test after being set 420 runs to score in their second innings. They were bowled out for 297.

Shiv sweeps - WI vs England.

Shiv in full flight.

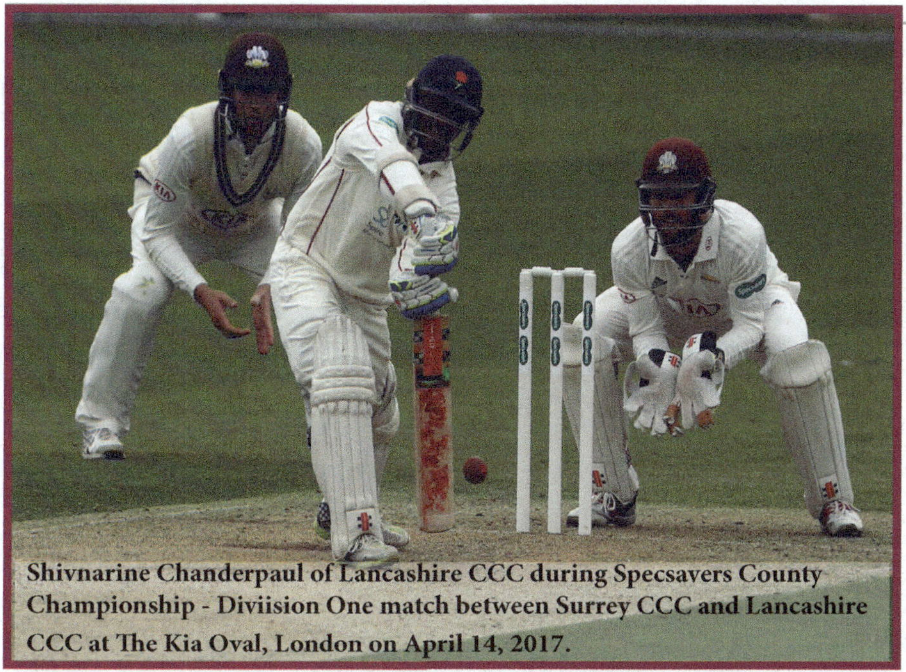
Shivnarine Chanderpaul of Lancashire CCC during Specsavers County Championship - Diviision One match between Surrey CCC and Lancashire CCC at The Kia Oval, London on April 14, 2017.

Shivnarine Chanderpaul hits the ball during the fourth day of the second NPower Cricket Test against England at Chester-le-Street in north-east England on May 17, 2009.

Shivnarine Chanderpaul (L) and captain Brian Lara run between wickets on the fifth and final day of the second test between India and West Indies at the Beausejour stadium in Gros Islet, St Lucia, 14 June 2006. West Indies, put to follow-on by India, are 83 runs for the loss of 3 wickets.

Shivnarine Chanderpaul drives a shot during a WI vs. Australia match.

Shivnarine Chanderpaul celebrates completing his century during the Group D match of the ICC World Cup Cricket 2007 between West Indies and Ireland at the Sabina Park Cricket Ground in Kingston, 23 March 2007. West Indies posted an easy 8 wickets victory over Ireland.

Shivnarine Chanderpaul, June 2008 VS AUS in Jamaica.

Shiv celebrates after a thrilling final ball .WI vs Sri Lanka in Trinidad (2008).

Shivnarine Chanderpaul and son, Tage, at practice in Guyana 2017.

Shivnarine plays at home for the Guyana Jaguars.

Shivnarine Chanderpaul vs. Sri Lanka at the Queen's Park Oval.

Shivnarine Chanderpaul WI vs. England 2009.

Shivnarine Chanderpaul 2012 VS AUS a Queen's Park Oval (Trinidad).

Shivnarine Chanderpaul WI vs India.

Shivnarine Chanderpaul vs. Sri Lanka at the Queen's Park Oval. (Trinidad).

West Indies top scorer (76 runs) Shivnarine Chanderpaul (R) goes for a boundary while England's Alec Stuart looks on, 19 December in Sharjah, during their Champions trophy final. England restricted West Indies to 235-7.

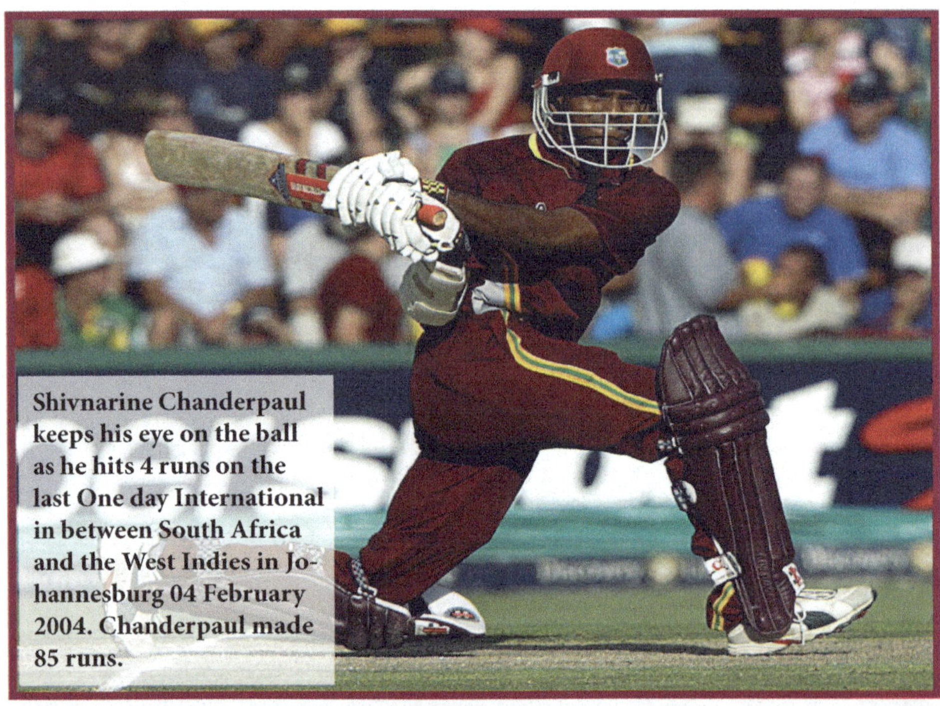

Shivnarine Chanderpaul keeps his eye on the ball as he hits 4 runs on the last One day International in between South Africa and the West Indies in Johannesburg 04 February 2004. Chanderpaul made 85 runs.

Shivnarine Chanderpaul sweeps at Queen's Park Oval (Trinidad).

Chapter 13

The Blossoming of a Batsman

Chanderpaul, displaying the sort of adaptability that has made him the West Indies most dependable batsman.

Wisden

Although the team was in decline, Shiv's progress as a batsman was encouraging. There were some times when the lack of support by his batting partners made Shiv's batting ineffective.

Early in the year 2007, before the English tour and the World Cup, India hosted to the West Indies in a contest comprising 4 ODIs. The series concluded with a 3-1 India victory but in the 3 matches in which Shiv played, he achieved scores of 149 n.o, 67 and 14, only failing in one innings. Wisden records that throughout, Shiv "showed the sort of adaptability that has made him the West Indies most dependable batsman". The signals he sent through the ODI success was evidence that he could have taken more risks in Test matches if all that mattered was his personal image. He repeatedly spoke of the team and the interest of the team. – "I am always thinking of the team, the players and how we respond to the difficult times," he recalls.

Shiv demonstrated superior skills compared with teammates, taking them close to victory in the first two matches. In Siddhartha Vaidyanathan's words, "he shone brighter than his teammates". In the first match as Vaidyanathan recounted Shiv "silenced the crowd with a violent start" though the team lost by 14 runs. He batted through the innings and on his performances was awarded Man of the Match. In the second ODI he again scored handsomely (67) but not with the flourishes of the first match. It was remarked that in the English encounters later in the year, Shiv proceeded to prove "an immovable object".

West Indies decline in performance as the years progressed was further exacerbated by the Board's ongoing war with the players and poor choices in team selection. Before and during this 2007 tour of England, burning issues were ongoing without any specific settlement. Matters were unresolved. However, the tour went on while their 'dispute went to arbitration'.

In addition to the on-going dispute with the Board, the failure in the 2007 World Cup, and the inexplicable loss to New Zealand, Lara found the constant battering and criticisms both unfair and intolerable. Lara's defence was the fact that problems lay in the quality of players he inherited. It was also a remark made by Sachin Tendulkar who had a fledgling team which took time to show their true potential. He then tendered his resignation. He was replaced as captain by Ramnaresh Sarwan.

Test 1 Eng	**553/5**	**Eng**	**437**	**Match drawn**
	284/8		**89/0**	

Test 2 Eng	**570/7**	**W.I**	**146**	**Eng won**
			141	
Test 3 Eng	**370**	**W.I**	**229**	**Eng won**
	313		**394**	
Test 4 W.I	**287**	**Eng**	**400**	**Eng won**
	222		**111/3**	

Shiv averaged 148.66 (1st placed) 2/100s 3/50s

The English tour proved disastrous as the West Indies suffered resounding defeats in three of their four Test series but managed a 2-1 victory in the ODIs and a drawn 1-1 T20 series. In a caustic commentary Stephen Brenkley remarked:

"It was business as usual for West Indies. Each day of their tour of England seemed to bring a fresh crisis, and when everyone felt it could get no worse, it got worse.' Brenkley here was referring to their new captain, Ramnaresh Sarwan's early departure due to shoulder injury, to the unresolved conflict between players and the WICB and he also knew that Lara's absence was a great loss to the team. There was also the fear that deficiencies evident in their quality of play and the dismal defeats could jeopardize their Test future as a Test playing country.

In the midst of it all, Shiv was described, in a Wisden report, as the last link with the great days of West Indies cricket who "performed the boy-on-the-burning-deck routine from start to finish". Handicapped with a knee injury (tendonitis), he limped through the tour courageously but missed the second Test. The great consolation for West Indies was their success in the ODI tournament with a 2-1 victory and a drawn T20 1-1 result. Brenkley noted "it gave the cricketing region something to cling to. There was still hope."

Sarwan's injury gave Daren Ganga an opportunity to lead the Test matches while Gayle was eventually given rein in the short matches. With all the numerous goings-on, one cricketer stood firm and unyielding in the execution of his craft.

In the opening Test for the Wisden Trophy at Lord's, England hoped to take advantage of Lara's absence. For the team, it was a void left by a player of considerable brilliance in his craft, and also one who was decisive and effective in his team's effort at victory. Still with the young Sarwan at the helm, they were bent on marshalling their forces for a competitive contest. On a dismal day with threatening clouds, Sarwan thought it prudent to let the English prove their mettle on a pitch that he thought would be of great assistance to his bowling squad. In fact, the bleak conditions were not fully exploited, partly due to the approach and resilience of the English opening pair. They weathered the storm and in the process, young Alastair Cook produced a century. This was followed by the support of the middle order batsmen who relished the more favourable conditions on the second day. The innings produced four centuries in a total of 553 with Collingwood, Prior and Bell gaining centuries in addition to Cook.

The West Indies reply was disappointing. Wickets fell periodically as they reached 187 for 5. Only Shiv's effort, combined with support from Bravo (56) and Ramdin (60), staved off a follow-on.

Wisden reporting on the match, praised Shiv's performance:

"He (Shiv) was at his obdurate best, batting for four and a half hours and taking his innings into the fourth day with a top score of 74. The grand efforts of Shiv, Bravo and Ramdin combined with some rear-guard action, took West Indies total to 437 but England then countered with a brisk 284 for 8 to give the West Indies a 401 target for victory in just over a day. England's captain, Andrew Strauss' decision was quite a sporting one, considering the fact that West Indies had successfully chased a 418 Australian total four years earlier. However, a rain interrupted last day put to rest any hope of a keen contest. A drawn match was the outcome."

The second Test proved disastrous as the West Indies were defeated in just over two days playing time; weather interruptions had stretched it to four days.

Shiv's tendonitis injury severely affected his batting. He said "I was bleeding under the right knee and as Panesar was bowling in the rough I could not play freely." Sarwan's shoulder injury during the match added to the West Indies problems. England's dominance was evident from the start. The dark grey skies and low temperature intensified West Indies' problems. An England total of 570/7 declared found no resistance as West Indies collapsed in both innings of 146 and 141. It was a loss by an innings and 283 runs – demoralizing and agonizing.

After the gloom of the 2nd Test, the third Test was more positive and more entertaining. There were some fine batting performances (229+394) and commendable bowling but not worthy enough to defeat a confident England, who set a target of 455. Harmison ploughed into the opening batsmen. West Indies mustered 394 but this was not competitive enough for victory. Here again, after Shiv's 50 in the first innings, he responded to England's total with 116 not out, running out of partners at the end to challenge England's total. Scyld Berry reports: "Chanderpaul needed no second invitation to occupy the crease; he had only got out the first time driving to extra-cover with the innings petering out. Often criticized for being one-paced, he scored his first 50 relatively quickly, but was unavoidably restricted as he accumulated his second 50 by Panesar bowling into the rough outside the off-stump." England's victory was a 60 run one.

Chester-Le-Street, the home of the Fourth Test, brought another victory for England by 7 wickets. It was another "comprehensive win against a hapless West Indies in three and a half days possible" on the rain-affected ground. It was remarked that "not even the redoubtable Chanderpaul, who battled for 11 hours over two innings in his guise as a one-man resistance force, could stop England".

With front line batsmen failing miserably (55 for 4) on a rain-drenched pitch, it was Shiv who "proved an immovable object," once again, scoring 136 not out It was only Bravo who showed courage as he partnered Shiv for two hours. An England response was foiled by Edwards as they were reduced to 165 for 6 but here again West Indies routinely let them off the hook. They eventually got to 400 and led by 113.

On the final day, it was now left to Shiv and Bravo after the fall of 3 wickets to restore some stability if they were to avoid defeat. Shiv scored 70 and Bravo 43 in a losing effort as Panesar 'breached the defences'. It was then left to the English batsmen to complete the destruction and this was done as anticipated.

Shiv was adjudged Man of the Match and West Indies Man Of The Series.

Wisden records:

"Panesar's last victim, to a missed sweep, was Chanderpaul, who had lasted 1,074 minutes (six minutes short of 18 hours) since his previous dismissal in the first innings at Old Trafford. It was the third time the limpet-like Chanderpaul had batted for more than 1,000 minutes between dismissals in Test cricket – he had survived 1,031 against Bangladesh and England in 2004, and a record 1,513 minutes against India in 2002. It was only the third time in 104 Tests that he had been bowled by a spinner: On his debut he had been bowled by Ian Salisbury, then in 1996 Shane Warne got him with one of his more miraculous leg-breaks."

West Indies still smarting from defeats, resumed the competition in the ODI version of the game. In the first ODI, chasing a target of 225, which was not beyond their capabilities, the early loss of captain Gayle caused some panic. At 13 for 4, Shiv entered. A sixth wicket partnership with Bravo yielded 61 runs but from then onwards Shiv watched dejectedly as a batting collapse brought agony to him. He was forced to eschew his attacking mode for careful and circumspect batting. He may have been circumspect but he never gave the bowlers the advantage. He witnessed Bravo's exit followed by Ramdin, Dwayne Smith and Darren Powell. It was only Rampaul who partnered him in a rear-guard stand of 35 as he contributed 24. Alas, he also went, leaving Shiv stranded with 10.1 overs to go. Here again, Shiv at 53 not out was the lone figure who stood his ground. His dominance and consistency made him a thorn to the English side. It was a saddened Shiv who walked off the pitch in gloom.

In his simple, innocent manner he attributed the loss to the inexperience of his teammates. Their failure had left him dejected but he described their performance as illustrative of lack of experience. In commenting on their failed efforts he said "I always try to guide them and build their confidence."

Of the second ODI at Edgbaston, Andrew McGlashan writes: "Inspired by another outstanding century from Shivnarine Chanderpaul, West Indies levelled the three-match One-Day series with a 61 run win at Edgbaston. Chanderpaul's unbeaten 116, and a third wicket stand of 175, formed the backbone of an impressive total as West Indies' final 10 overs brought 102 runs."

West Indies reversed the first ODI result in the second encounter with a solid platform which was exploited fully and sensibly by Shiv and Samuel who both launched an aggressive assault. In a score of 278 for 5, Samuel showed his mettle as a batsman as he lit up the last 10 overs with his brilliance. He carved 77 not out to his credit. Shiv, in partnership, worked his way to an 85 ball 50 but then accelerated his score. It took 29 balls to complete his century. With good company he was able to be audacious with rich and diverse strokeplay. It was evident here that his loyalty to team was significant. It was a partnership of daring, of perfect timing as both batsmen wielded their willows in their dispatches to the boundary. Both batsmen energized their innings with flourishes which entertained and also propelled their team to victory.

Shiv and Samuel established a third wicked stand of 125 – his contribution was 116 not out and Samuel 77 not out. This was Shiv's 9th ODI century and has been described as 'a perfect paced innings of 122 balls".

"Chanderpaul proved he could attack in one-day games as brilliantly as he could defend in Test cricket. The innings accelerated as he contributed 116 not out of 122 balls with 3 sixes and 9 fours," was Wisden's report.

England's response was 217 with no one establishing a dominant innings as Ravi Rampaul made a career best 4-41.

In the last ODI at Trent Bridge, West Indies once more dominated with a 93 runs victory. The batting performance spear-headed by Gayle (82) and Morton (82 not out) propelled the team to a score of 289 for 5. This total was good motivation for the teammates' confidence, particularly the bowlers. England replied modestly (196) with only a brief counter-attack. What was interesting was the perception of Shiv's presence in the team. In light of this, it is curious to note McGlashan's comment: "the most pleasing aspect about this innings for West Indies was that

Shivnarine Chanderpaul contributed only 33- a relative failure given the riches of the tour – but others stood up to take the slack." Here it was a vibrant, spirited display by all teammates who took advantage of a positive start by the batsmen.

HIGHEST TEST SERIES AVERAGE BY AN OVER-SEAS BATSMAN IN ENGLAND

(MINIMUM THREE TESTS)

Avg.	T	I	NO	Runs	HS	100s	
148.66 S.Chanderpaul (W.I.)	3	5	2	446	136*	2	2007
139.14 D.G. Bradman (Australia)	5	7	0	974	334	4	1930
126.50 S.R. Waugh (Austalia)	6	8	4	506	177*	2	1989
118.42 I.V.A Richards (W.I.)	4	7	0	829	291	3	1976
108.56 D.G.Bradman (Australia)	4	6	2	434	144*	3	1938
107.00 S.R.Waugh (Australia)	4	5	2	321	157*	2	2001
103.14 G.S.Sobers(W.I.)	5	8	1	722	174	3	1966
100.66 V.Pollard (New Zeland)	3	5	2	302	116	2	1973
100.33 R.Dravid (India)	4	6	0	602	217	3	2002

Chapter 14

Rare Consistency

"The immovable object"

A bitter sense of frustration intensified among the West Indian spectating public with the team's continuing failures at international level. It was a team blanched into insignificance- a team bereft of distinguished campaigners. No more was there the bludgeoning deliveries of Roberts, Hall, Holding, Marshall, Croft, Garner, Ambrose and Walsh among others who once were the refrain of supporters. No more the supreme batsmanship of Sobers, Worrell, Richards, Kanhai and more recently, Lara. This was the agony of defeat for a population that once stood proud in the latter part of the 20th century.

The cricket season of December 2007 continuing to the end of 2008 was not very different from the previous years. The South African tour (Dec 2007) began on a deceptive note as the West Indies team in defiance of dull expectations, won the first Test at Port Elizabeth by 128 runs. As Wisden notes: "West Indies recorded their first win at Port Elizabeth in South Africa, their first anywhere for 31 months, and the first overseas outside Zimbabwe and Bangladesh since beating England at Edgbaston in June 2000".

Neil Manthorp who covered the tour remarked: "Caribbean joy at the start of the tour was great enough to spark talk of a renaissance of West Indies fortunes." At the end of the tour, it was a down-trodden West Indies team, having lost 1-2 in the Test tournament, 0-5 in the ODI's and a consolation 1-1 in the T20's.

In the midst of defeat, Shiv, one of the few combatants in the team, emerged with Test scores of 104, 65 n.o, 70 n.o in two Tests but illness caused his retirement in the second innings of the third Test.

At Cape Town, West Indies suffered their second loss by seven wicket and at Durban it was disastrous for the West Indies as South Africa emerged with winning by an innings and 100 runs. Though Shiv achieved his 17th Test century, he was heavily criticized for his doggedness but "effective obduracy". The descriptive word 'immovable' characterized many of his 'stubborn' innings. This immovability led South Africa captain Graeme Smith to agonize, "He's like a tick you can't get rid of. He doesn't kill you, he just wears you down."

Test 1 W.I	**408**	**SA**	**195**	**W.I won**
	175		**260**	
Test 2 W.I	**243**	**SA**	**321**	**SA won**
	262		**186/3**	
Test 3 W.I	**139**	**SA**	**556/4**	**SA won**
	317			

Shiv averaged 82.33 (1st placed) 1/100 2/50s

Shiv had made his seventh consecutive 50 in Test cricket, a record shared by only Everton Weekes and Andy Flower. At the end of the tour, he emerged with an average of 82.33 – exactly 30.00 above the second highest average (52.33) of Marlon Samuels.

The West Indian team returned home in early 2008 to battle Sri Lanka, with the hope of gaining supremacy at home. However, crowd participation in the Test was minimal; it was only apparent when there seemed signs of an interesting climax. While each team shared 1-1 victories, the One Days were dominated by the West Indies. The Tests brought to the fore major contributions from Vaas and Murali vs Chanderpaul and Sarwan. This series was expressive of Sarwan's skill and talent and also Shiv's confident batting and reliability.

Test 1 SL	**476/8**	**W.I**	**280**	**SL won**
	240/7		**315**	
Test 2 W.I	**278**	**SL**	**294**	**W.I won**
	268		**254/4**	

Sarwan had returned after injury without the responsibility of captaincy and now played under Gayle. His successes led one to presume that the freedom from the burden of captaincy gave him the freedom to adventure. All his four Test innings were in excess of 50 – 80, 72, 52, 102. In Tony Cozier's words: "His 80 and 72 in the first Test were not quite enough to prevent defeat; his 57 and more especially his 102 in the second Test guaranteed victory."

The Tests also reminded us once again of Shiv's numerous contributions to the team. In the second Test in attempting to challenge 253 for victory, signs of despair were apparent as the top order collapsed (73-3) as before lunch, Gayle, Chattergoon and Samuels were banished to the dressing room. It was then that the two adventurous combatants, Shiv and Sarwan, took up the challenge amidst growing unease and tension. A partnership of 157 in response showed "calm confidence and character." Both emerged with scores (Sarwan 102 and Shiv 86 no) in their victory chase. Together with Devon Smith, Shiv brought home victory.

Wisden aptly summarizes the significance of the outcome of the second Test:

There was silent despair as they slipped to 73 for 3 before lunch. Amid rising tension, Sarwan and Chanderpaul, their likeliest survivors, proceeded to reverse the team's habit of snatching defeat from the jaws of victory with a stand of 157, full of calm confidence and character.

In this tour, Shiv's three meagre scores of 23,3 and 18 were followed by three significant innings which brought victory to the West Indies. In Test two, his unbroken stand of 86 steered West Indies to victory. This was followed by the dramatic win in the last two balls of the first ODI when he dealt Vass two stinging blows, 4 and 6 needed by his team. Tony Cozier commented that such as exciting end to the match, "made the point that 50-overs cricket might yet survive the challenge of Twenty 20."

Shiv recalls his share of discomfort during the innings though he was able to bring victory. The wicket, he said, "was slow and turning. I was unwell and weak but I had to stay and struggle to the end. I got support from Bravo and Taylor to ease the pressure on me. When we needed the runs during the last over I saw people walking away as if they could not handle the tension. But also there was loud music from the stands and this gave me energy to play aggressively. What amazed me was the atmosphere. It was encouraging and this helped me to stay and plan my attack. It's a game that will be always remembered as it came down to the wire."

It was a momentous occasion at Queen's Park Oval, Trinidad. The emotions of tension, anxiety, heart-throbbing moments, excitement and thrill filled the air. The animation and sense of vitality in Shiv's response to Vaas' bowling was exceedingly enthralling. Roars of laughter, tears of joy and a spirit of delight spread across the stands as spectators seemed loathe to leave the pavilion. The joy expressed itself in music as the fans "tossed their heads in sprightly dance". Those moments have remained in the memory and are related repeatedly by those passionate viewers of the match. Such moments defy time, transcend time and remain eternal. It is reminiscent of Sunil Gavaskar's dramatic impact in the Caribbean which inspired a calypso in his honour and which remains popular even after 50 years since its first rendition. The ovation was lavish when he returned to his homeland after his successful tour. Such moments – Shiv's dramatic win over Sri Lanka, Gavaskar's memorable career in the West Indies, Yuvraj Singh's record six sixes and Lara's record-breaking scores – among others – make the game enduring.

In the second ODI, Shiv's 52 not out helped West Indies in

their thrust for victory.

Shiv was able to adjust to the varying situations he encountered. He met successfully the challenges of concentration and application. His thought and judgement enabled him to succeed against the variables of opposing attacks, using nimbleness, dexterity and presence of mind to counter their bowling effectively. His response to the challenge was indicative of his competitive spirit. At the conclusion, he was named Man of the Series.

Though well-reputed for their fluctuating fortunes, particularly at Test level, the WI emerged admirably in the Test encounters with Australia in 2008, despite defeat.

Alex Brown, in his Wisden report, noted that "from a gladiatorial perspective, there was no more engrossing sight than that of Brett Lee, the irresistible force, charging in to Chanderpaul, the immovable object. Here were two giants of the modern game, both at the height of their powers and called upon to shoulder responsibilities far in excess of their job descriptions. As team mates fall around them….. the pain rose to each challenge, carrying with them the aspirations of their teams."

In the West Indies' first innings at Sabina, Lee's devastating bouncer knocked the back of Chanderpaul's helmet. The knock on Shiv's helmet was terrifying to all who looked on. Shiv said "my eyes were blurred and I was conscious. I did not hit the stump or stay out the crease. I felt paralyzed and told the physio to massage my arms and legs. I heard Ricky Ponting say - He can't bat anymore. Take the guy inside. Ponting probably felt they had got rid of me for the innings."

Shiv's response was warrior-like, though the blow numbed his body for a while. His response was indicative of his courage and fortitude as he continued to resist whatever was thrown at him until he reached 118, last man out. His response to Lee's pace after the blow, was truly a testament of his prowess as a batsman. Alex Brown commented that Shiv summoned "untold levels of courage".

Throughout his career his response to any opposition was incredible to critics. That he could withstand the onslaught of varied bowling attacks for hours was indicative of the quality of his batsmanship. He would face his adversary with either aggression or obduracy. As the tour progressed, Shiv was in command.

Australia's 431 was met with an early West Indian collapse and it was left to Shiv coupled with Morton and Bravo to attain 312 amidst a mesmerizing piece of pace. In the second innings, WI capitulated and Australia took the honours.

Test 1 Aus	**431**	**W.I**	**312**	**Aus won**
	167		**191**	
Test 2 Aus	**479/7**	**W.I**	**352**	**Match drawn**
	244/6		**266/5**	
Test 3 Aus	**251**	**W.I**	**216**	**Aus won**
	439/5		**387**	

Shiv averaged 147.33 (1st placed) 2/100s 3/50s
Man of the Series

In the first innings of the second Test, both Sarwan and Shiv frustrated Australia's attempt to secure a second victory. Again Shiv's presence was dominant as he scored another century (107 no). He faced 236 deliveries but was bereft of a partner at his score of 107. It was his defiance that was admirable.

In the second innings, once more Shiv in concert with Sarwan weathered the storm. Both were 'rarely unsettled' in their partnership which lasted 53 overs with a score of 143runs between them. Shiv was firm as he withstood the on- slaughter of 180 deliveries in his score of 77 no. The Man of the Match award was befitting to his achievement.

The third Test was also a combat in which Shiv again tried to rebuild a losing battle from 108 for 4; West Indies eventually got to 216 in response to 251. Shiv (79 n.o) was again left partnerless. Australia's second innings of 439 was dominant, giving West Indies a high target of 475 for victory. It is interesting to note that this target was not impossible and could have been the highest target – if achievable – to win a match.

The dynamic partnership between DJ Bravo and Shiv seemed hopeful for a West Indian thrust for victory and this would have given Ricky Ponting some degree of fear after his 418 loss in 2003. Bravo was aggressive as he punished Casson for 3 powerful sixes which enticed the crowd into revelry but then conceded his wicket carelessly. This gave Australia a great sense of hope and they eventually trapped Shiv at his score of 50. This was Shiv's first dismissal since the second innings of the first Test. The other batsmen offered little resistance and ended the innings 87 short of victory. It was a match that was in the making for an exciting finish. The series ended with a 2-0 Australian victory.

At the end of the series Shiv had scored 442 runs, gaining an average of 147.33.Wisden states that Shiv faced "exactly 1000 balls, an effort that went a long way towards earning him the ICC Cricketer of the year award which is named after another West Indian left hander, Sir Gary Sobers".

The second batsman in line was Sarwan with an average of 45.83. Shiv, at the end of this series, also joined the band of consistent performers who had most often averaged 100+ in a series of three or more Tests.

CONSISTENT PERFORMERS

Batsmen most often averaging at least 100 in a series of three or more Tests:

Javed Miandad(P) v. NZ 1976-77; v E 1977-78; v I 1978-79; v I 1982-83; SL 1985-86.

R. T. Ponting (A) v I 199-2000; v WI 2002-03+; v I 2003-2004; v P 2004-05; v SA 2005-06.

D. G. Bradman (A) v E 1930+; v SA 1931-32; v E 1938+; v I 1947-48.

G. Sobers (WI) v P 1957-58: v E 1959-60; v E 1966+; v I 1966-67+.

S. R. Tendulkar (I) v E 1992-93; v SL 1993-94+; v A 1997-98; v NZ 1990-2000.

S. R Waugh (A) v E 1989+; v NZ 1993-4; v WI 1994-95+; E 2001+.

S. Chanderpaul (WI) v I 2001-02; v E 2007+; v A 2007-2008.

Shiv's form continued into the Pakistan ODI encounters in Abu Dhabi when he struck another century. At the same time, West Indies fortunes were declining. Pakistan won the 3 ODI matches.

Almost to the point of ridicule, Tony Cozier describes West Indies' engagement with New Zealand (in the tour that followed) in 2008 as a 'fly weight bout'. Cozier alluded at the same time to the level of decadence in West Indies cricket performance. It was a mini-two Test series spoilt by rainy conditions.

In the One-Days New Zealand got the better results (2-1) but West Indies was able to draw the T20s encounters (1-1). The Tests were drawn 0-0.

Test 1 NZ	**365**	**W.I 340 Match drawn**	
	44/2		
Test 2 W.I	**307**	**NZ 371 Match drawn**	
	375		**220/5**

Shiv 1/100 1/50

At the conclusion, West Indies remained 7th in the Test rankings. Apart from Bangladesh and Zimbabwe (two of the lesser mortals in cricket) West Indies had not won one away series since 1994-95.

In this New Zealand series there was heavy dependence on their two most experienced players. In the first Test, Gayle made an aggressive 74 while Shiv dropped anchor as the innings started to falter. He supported Jerome Taylor as he showed his mettle with a maiden Test hundred. Shiv's contribution was 74, but it was a drawn contest as rain affected the outcome. Shiv remarked that he played second fiddle to Jerome Taylor so he could reach a century. After Jerome's exit Shiv tried to accelerate and in the process he did not attain a century.

In terms of match figures, New Zealand batting first had secured a total of 365. In response, after the poor response of 173 for six, Shiv and Taylor rescued the team to a reasonable 340, within sight of New Zealand's total. But during New Zealand's response, the weather intervened to end the proceedings.

Shiv took care of the first innings of the second Test with 126 n.o in a total of 307, then Gayle dominated the second innings with a masterful 197; it was entertaining but had no effect on the outcome. At 74 for 4 in the first innings, Shiv again had to steer the ship when the front-line batsmen were eliminated. It was only BP Nash who lent support with 74 in their thrust to accumulate a formidable score. Shiv may have appeared stubborn but he took his time to salvage some respectability to the score and at the same time completed his 20th Test century.

Chapter 15

Shiv's Ascent in World Cricket

As the first decade of the millennium moved towards its end (2009), Tony Cozier in his Wisden commentary describes the decade as turbulent. For him and most scribes, "West Indian cricket plummeted inexorably towards irrelevance, perhaps even towards demise". But a bright light did shine amidst the darkness when West Indies regained the Wisden Trophy during an interesting series in February/March of 2009 in the Caribbean.

A series of five Test matches culminated with a 1-0 West Indian victory, 1-0 in the T20 but a 2-3 defeat in the One-Day Internationals. What was remarkable was the dramatic routing of the English from a fiery spell of fast bowling (5 for 11) off Jerome Taylor's effort in the first Test at Sabina Park, Jamaica. It was disastrous and demoralizing for the English team. The West Indies won by an inning and 23 runs and in the process had decimated the English team for 51 runs, their third lowest total.

Test 1	**Eng**	**318**	**W.I**	**392**	**W.I won**
		51			
Test 2 Aborted (Eng 7/0)					
Test 3	**Eng**	**566/9**	**W.I**	**285**	**Match drawn**

	221/8		**370/9**	
Test 4 Eng	**600/6**	**W.I**	**749**	**Match drawn**
	279/2			
Test 5 Eng	**546/6**	**W.I**	**544**	**Match drawn**
	237/6		**114/8**	

Shiv averaged 59.80 (2nd placed) 1/100 2/50s

The critics will remind us of the West Indian/English battles which will linger on in the memory. There are memories of Ambrose's 6 for 24 when he demoralized the English team at the Queen's Park Oval in the 93-94 series. In this match he had dismissed England for 46, their second lowest total. The cricket fraternity at Sabina Park would also remember Steve Harmison's 7 for 12 in 2003-2004. The West Indies team could only muster 47 runs, their lowest total on record.

This series was dominated by Ramnaresh Sarwan's achievements with the bat also boosted by Shiv's scores of 70, 55, 147 in Test matches, and 112 not out in the One-Day Internationals.

The first Test of this series proved an interesting and dramatic encounter. First innings performance was close in accomplishments with the West Indies gaining a 74 run lead advantage; England's 318 was set against West Indies 392. In this first innings, the Sabina pitch had shown no great terror in pace bowling and this was unusual. Sixty-eight overs were delivered by the gentle offerings of Gayle and Benn and, on the other hand, England produced 51 overs of gentle pace.

In the second innings, with England's front line batsmen seeking to overcome the lead and proceed to generate a creditable score which would have challenged the West Indies batsmen, there was "no indication of a coming disaster", (an echo of the description of the destruction of Port Royal) as Jerome Taylor's burst of aggression decimated the English front line order between lunch and tea. Fast and full of length, Taylor dismissed Andrew Strauss (9), Cook (0), Pieterson (1), Collingwood (1) and Prior (0). It was an evening which shocked the English into sadness and dismay. Taylor's 5 for 11 added to his first innings scalps of 3 for 74.

Mayhem is the word to describe the scene at Sabina; it brought joy and thrill to a spectating public eager for dynamic cricket but it also reminded the cognoscenti of West Indies' dismal display six years earlier when Harmison had scorched the West Indian batting in his 7 for 12 performance.

The match needed no West Indian second innings as the English were reduced to scores not exceeding West Indies' first innings total. It was an innings and 23 runs defeat. In West Indies batting performance, Sarwan's 107 and Gayle's 104 were the major contributions. Shiv's, (Mr. Reliable) contribution was insignificant in the context of the outcome of the match.

Antigua suffered the humiliation of an abandoned second Test due to inadequate preparation, but tried feverishly to host the third Test in the same island, moving from the abandoned North Sound location to a former Test ground, the Antigua Recreation Ground. It was a great challenge to host the third Test in Antigua but the effort was successful and the match was played.

As an historical fact, the Antigua Recreation Ground is famous for its high scoring run fest. It was here that Brian Lara created history with his record breaking 375 to surpass Sir Gary Sobers 365 and earn the world record for the highest individual Test score followed by 400 not out, his second record breaking feat, surpassing Mathew Hayden's 380 highest Test Score.

In the third Test, England amassed a mammoth total of 566 and followed up in the second innings with 221; this 221/8 was a total not reflecting the batting performance but due to the exigencies of the match. The West Indian response of 285 was not commendable on such a ground; they followed up with 370 for 9, staving off a defeat. The two batsmen, Sarwan (106) and Shiv (55) together with lower order resisted the English efforts and earned a draw in this Test.

The fourth Test at the Kensington Oval was dominated by the bat over the ball. England accumulated 600 for 6 and 279 for 2 as against West Indies run fest of 749. The match petered out into a drawn Test. Scyld Berry laments a pitch that gave everything to batsman on which Sarwan (291) lasted 698 minutes and Ramdin (166) 424 minutes.

Had Chanderpaul (70) not been given out due to a blatant umpiring error, (hit well above the outside leg), Berry exclaims, he "could have batted a week."

The fifth and final Test at the Queen's Park Oval, Port of Spain, has been described by Ian Bishop as "largely mundane" but "culminating in a gripping contest" with tail-end Fidel Edwards stubbornly resisting the last over to avoid what could have been a West Indian defeat. This Test also produced prolific scores on both sides, each scoring in excess of 500.

Pursuing a first innings target of 546, Shiv and Nash brought up a total of 544 (2 runs short of England's). Ian Bishop notes that "It was fitting that Chanderpaul accompanied Nash to his maiden Test hundred during a vital partnership of 234, a fifth wicket record on this ground. Nash had made no secret of his reverence for Shiv's approach to batting; not only did he incorporate some of Shiv's characteristics into his own game, he was slightly more fluent."

In the One-Day Internationals, West Indies were defeated 2-3 in the five matches. It is fitting to remember Shiv's role in the second ODI in which West Indies posted 264 for 8 which was unmatched by England. In company with Sarwan, Shiv's innings of 112 not out was one of skill and dexterity and creative batting. ESPN Cricinfo reports: "When Strauss set a deep off-side field he hit over the leg side; when the gap was plugged, he backed away and went over mid-off. Shiv had the confidence to bring out the reverse sweep against Broad and repeated the dose against the medium pace of Mascarenhas and Collingwood."

In Shiv's innings he demonstrated mastery over the varied attack. With ease and poise and timeless grace, he wielded his willow with perfect strokes. In this match he became the third West Indies batsman to pass 8000 ODI runs. This feat had been achieved by only two others, Brian Lara and Desmond Haynes.

In the midst of the cricketing agenda and schedules for match play, Cozier comments on the characteristic controversy and confrontation beyond the boundary that has long shaped the feelings within it. The catalyst was the prolonged hostility between the West Indies Cricket Board and the West Indies Players Association, principally over retainer contracts in 2009.

Tony Cozier continues in his candid report on the turbulence that affected adversely West Indian cricket performances and its image in the cricketing world.

"There was disagreement as well over a brief, hastily arranged return series in England in May that the players felt had been foisted on them, prompting a virtual go-slow and the immediate surrender of the Wisden Trophy. No creative urges seemed to flow as they seemed drained, dry, sterile in execution. By July, the issues had developed into a full-blown strike by the leading players – the second in four years – reducing the home rubber against Bangladesh to a farce. A team of unprepared and inexperienced reserves was quickly gathered together but lost both Tests and all three One-Day Internationals. Retained for the subsequent Champions Trophy, they predictably lost all three matches.

It took the intervention of the relevant governments of Caricom, (the regional alliance), to secure a grudging, provisional agreement that ended the stand-off, returned the strikers to the fold, and allowed the selection of a full-strength team for the series in Australia".

The return bout with England was hastily planned and executed in May of the same year. The West Indies Cricket Board was all too willing to accommodate the tour with the prospect of a handsome monetary package. The outcome of the short series was described as 'yet another debacle'.

The West Indies suffered a monumented loss in the two-match series, particularly so when they had won the Wisden Trophy two months earlier. Within three days England had demolished the West Indian team - a loss by 10 wickets at Lord's. Then at Chester-Le-Street, a market town in Durham Country, West Indies succumbed once more - an innings and 83 runs defeat. This meant a surrender of the Wisden Trophy after two months of retrieving it in the Caribbean. The humiliation was compounded with the loss of both One-Day Internationals.

Test 1 Eng	**377**	**W.I**	**152**	**Eng won**
	32/0		**256**	
Test 2 Eng	**569/6**	**W.I**	**310**	**Eng won**
			176	

In the Australian encounter later in the year, November/ December 2009, West Indies went down in flames, although there were some brilliant sparks that made West Indies cricket look beautiful. But this diminished too quickly for a West Indian audience which hungered for victory. Since February 1997, West Indies had not gained a victory in Australia. In this series, signs of another defeat looked imminent after they lost the first Test by an innings - in three days at the Gabba.

Test 1 Aus	**480/8**	**W.I**	**228**	**Aus won**
			187	
Test 2 W.I	**451**	**Aus**	**439**	**Match drawn**
	317		**212/5**	
Test 3 Aus	**520/7**	**W.I**	**312**	**Aus won**
	150		**323**	

Despite the loss of the three – Test series (2-0), there was some promise from Kemar Roach (age 21) whose aggression with pace flustered the veteran skipper and outstanding batsman, Ricky Ponting. In addition to this, 19-year old Adrian Barath's debut century brought delight and hope to the West Indian cricketing fraternity who yearned for a West Indies resurgence.

It was a series in which West Indies accumulated more centuries and totalled more runs than Australia but were not victorious. Barath, Bravo and Gayle's two centuries were set against a victorious Australian team which managed eight half-centuries. No Australian reached the century mark. West Indian performance in batting led critics to surmise about revival.

The first Test was another soul-searcher for the West Indies' players who suffered an innings and 65 runs defeat within three days. Apart from Barath's 104, TM Dowlin's 62 and Ramdin's 54, all other batsmen including Gayle and Shiv failed. But the second Test at Adelaide brought some vibrancy and dynamism to the series with Gayle's "monolithic unbeaten 165 at Adelaide", D. J. Bravo's century (104) B.P Nash's 92, and 24, Shiv's 62 and 27. The highlight was Gayle's innings, though Chanderpaul was the 'cornerstone'. Shiv's four-hour 62 ended with a controversial decision.

Wisden reports: "Chanderpaul was the cornerstone, with a four-hour stand that ended in controversial circumstances when the third umpire, Asad Rauf, ruled in favour of Australia after a referral, claiming that "common sense" enabled him to deduce the faintest of edges when the technology was not able to pick up the contact. The on-field umpire, Mark Benson, withdrew from the match that night and flew straight home to England. Many observers speculated that his decision was driven by Rauf overruling him, although Benson later released a statement claiming he was ill and unable to see out the Test."

That incident sparked off great debate and ire from the West Indian public. It was felt that Shiv's contribution would have been of great impact on the match had he continued in support of Gayle's assault on the Australian bowling.

Wisden, in its report, highlights that the West Indian spirit was lifted by their performance in the third Test at Perth, and although Australia clinched the series with another victory, West Indies' efforts brought them close to a drawn series as they were 36 short of the Australian target. Responding to a target of 359, West Indies fell short by 36 runs. It was remarked by Wisden that "the absence of Chanderpaul (forced to withdraw because of a finger damaged at Adelaide) and of the teenager revelation Adrian Barath, (who had torn a hamstring doing extra fitness sessions), proved crucial".

In an appropriate critical summation of the series, John Townsend remarked: "A series that started with a whimper of West Indian woes ended with the alleged basket-case of world cricket getting within 36 runs of squaring the three-test rubber against an Australian team whose behaviour deteriorated the more they were placed under pressure."

Wisden reports: The result flattered Australia, who dominated the early going in the series when their opponents were reeling from a limited and disrupted preparation and were run over in the middle stages, and came back in stuttering bursts at the end. And it took a questionable decision from third umpire Asad Rauf, already a contentious figure for overruling Mark Benson at Adelaide with what he himself described as "common sense" and a "gut feeling" rather than any technological clarification, to get the home team over the line."

Wisden in 2009 introduced a Test XI (The first eleven) based on cricketers' performances of each year. The following piece explains the selection process.

THE WISDEN TEST XI

The First Eleven

SCYLD BERRY

We introduce the Wisden Test XI. The aim is to recognize the best Test cricketers of the calendar year, and to endorse Test cricket as the highest, most skilled form of the game, and the least subject to the intrusion of time.

The criteria for selections are simple; the best eleven to play a Test match, no matter the opposition, guided by performances in 2008, and taking into consideration the amount of Test cricket they played in the year, the quality of their opponents, and that indefinable blend of class and form.

The following paragraph explains briefly Shivnarine Chanderpaul's selection.

Shivnarine Chanderpaul was another unanimous choice. As Bishop put it: sheer weight of runs and a great strength of character make him a no-brainer for this team. It is a phenomenal effort to average over 100 in Tests in a year, and Chanderpaul made it his second in a row. (He averaged 111.60 in 2007, and 101 in 2008.)

Ravi Shastri noted that "he glues the lower order and makes runs in all conditions, from seaming pitches in England to spitting turners in Asia and indifferent tracks at home."

THE WISDEN TEST XI OF 2008

V. Sehway (India

G.C. Smith (South Africa)

R.T. Ponting (Australia)

S.R. Tendulkar (India)

K. P. Pietersen (England)

S. Chanderpaul (West Indies)

M. S. Dhoni (India)

Harbhajan Singh (India)

M.G. Johnson (Australia)

D.W. Steyn (South Africa)

Zaheer Khan (India)

Chapter 16

A Gentleman's Game Abused

The type of behaviour that diminishes man as a social being.

Michael Manley

In the Australia tour at the beginning of 2010, the absence of Shiv, Dwayne Bravo, Sarwan and Taylor through injuries was partly responsible for a return to disaster. On that score there was a fair degree of public sympathy for the team. In both format of the game, the One-Day International and the T20, Australia demonstrated their prowess.

In the first ODI, Australia's 113 run victory set the tone for the ODI's. The Australian took complete control by vanquishing the visitors with authority. This defeat was then followed by a pathetic start by West Indies in the second match which Australia won by eight wickets. In the third encounter, rain caused play to be abandoned. A scintillating century by Ricky Ponting in Match 4 delighted the home crowed and in Match 5 the winning formula was again effective.

After the ODI matches, 'sizzling spells' of fast bowling and batting which bludgeoned the West Indians, victory for Australia was achieved in both T20 matches. An almost startling discovery was the depleted numbers in attendance; the West Indian failures were no encouragement for the crowd's energetic interest and response.

The crowd at a match is integral to the spirit that pervades. They add drama through their delight and laughter, smiles and banter but deep down there is a passion that stimulates them, a passion that drives their spirit and engulfs their very being. The vitality and progress of each team adds life to the game as the game is not only played out in the field but amongst an audience seeking joy and pride in their team's success. They bring radiance and light to the game, a sense of solidarity on each rival's side, particularly among West Indian and Indian crowds. In the Caribbean, the crowds have suffered for 20 years, the ignominy of defeats more than the pleasures of success. As a result the crowds have diminished, their interest waned and engendered sadness in the region. Even in the games now, during Covid 19 without an audience, there is a void that diminishes the delight and interest that a match provides. In these shorter versions of the game, Australia's superiority was commanding against the mediocrity and unimpressive display of rivalry.

Of serious concern was the subsequent encounter with Zimbabwe in the Caribbean in February/March 2010. The alarm bell was deafening when the West Indians were defeated in the first two matches even after they energized themselves enough to capture the remaining four.

In summary, the results show Zimbabwe won the first T20 by 26 runs and the first ODI by two runs. The remaining 4 matches were in West Indies favour. With Shiv once more in the team, his run-a-ball 70 in the second ODI proved essential and his 58 off 76 deliveries in the third ODI provided the response needed to establish victories to clinch the series.

To the critics and analysts and West Indian spectating public, victories over Zimbabwe did not point to improvement. Further demise followed.

The descent was more evident and more pronounced when the May/June 2010 South African contingent presented themselves for a mixed series of T20, One Days and Tests. Save for one drawn Test match, West Indies lost every engagement with the South Africans. West Indian cricket fans were terribly disappointed with their team, and this was evident by their absence except for the two One Days.

Test 1 SA	**352**	**W.I**	**102**	**SA won**
	206/4		**293**	
Test 2 SA	**543/6**	**W.I**	**546**	**Match drawn**
	235/3			
Test 3 W.I	**231**	**SA**	**346**	**SA won**
	161		**49/3**	

Shiv averaged 75.00 (1st placed) 1/100 1/50

Fidel Edwards, Adrian Bharath, Ramnaresh Sarwan and Jerome Taylor sustained injuries of one kind or another. This put the West Indies further at the mercy of the in-form South Africans.

The disparity between the two teams was most evident in the Tests. Dale Steyn and Morne Morkel presented problems with the new ball as the batsmen faltered. Steyn won the Man of the Series for taking 15 wickets, – using aggression and the reverse swing. The 6ft 6", Morkel was able to get the ball to bounce on docile pitches and took 14 wickets.

The first Test concluded with one day to spare as South Africa 'surge to victory'. On a docile pitch, Steyn and Morkel exploited the West Indies batting with fiery and aggressive pace. It was as though the pacemen were 'summoning their courage with hard favoured rage, lending the eye a terrible aspect' to intimidate the batsmen. This attitude was very evident in the confrontation between Steyn and Benn. Another negative that sullies the noble tenets of the game is the robust sledging that is aimed at intimidating the batsmen at the crease. The critics always proclaim: 'It's not cricket,' and the game which is intended to show character and noble values has become diminished in spirit of delight through flaws in many characters. Their rage reveals their lack of humaneness. Michael Manley describes this as a "type of behaviour that diminishes man as a social being".

Fragility in the batting was most apparent as evident in a meagre 102 response to a formidable 352 by South Africa. The match petered out with a lack of enthusiasm, particularly as the West Indian team were without their pacemen, Edwards, Taylor and Roach due to injuries. This was compounded by injuries to Sarwan and Bharat.

Mammoth totals in Test 2 at St Kitts only prompted a tame draw. There were five days of 'batting on by both teams in front of a sparse audience'. Facing a formidable 543, West

Indies batsmen asserted themselves, in particular Shiv and Brandon Nash, following Gayle's and Deonarine's contributions. Both Shiv and Nash achieved centuries. With a 'counter-attacking 220 in 200 minutes, they were able to surpass the South Africa total by 3 runs. South Africa's total of 543/6 was countered by a West Indies 546. A second innings South Africa 235/3 was the response at the end. It was Shiv's 15th Test century but before he could achieve it, he was felled by a Steyn bouncer. Though Steyn continued hustling down the pitch, Shiv stood with calm composure.

In the third Test, a fragile batting display by the West Indies (231) meant another defeat by 7 wickets. The 'clinical opponents' had demolished the batting line-up with only Shiv's (71 not out) counter attack in the second innings of any value. Sadly, his attempts to anchor the batting came to naught as the rest of the team succumbed to South Africa's bowling armoury.

A series already demoralizing to the West Indies team was blemished by unsportsmanly behaviour by both teams. A game reputed for its civility and dignity was trampled upon by insolence and arrogance.

The following piece records the unsavory incidents.

"South Africa thus took the series 2-0, and made the overall score 9-0 in ten international matches on their tour. The outcome, however, was sullied by incidents on the last two days, on and off the field, which resulted in heavy fines for Steyn and Roach, and Benn's second suspension in six months under ICC's Code of Conduct.

As Steyn walked away after he was bowled by Roach in the first innings, he spat in the direction of the taunting Benn who had laughed derisively as he passed. Steyn's coarse response drew a fine from his complete match fee. But Benn hadn't let the matter rest and entered the South Africans' dressing-room during lunch to accost players and management. His punishment, following a complaint from the South Africans, was a suspension of one Test (or two limited-overs games, whichever came next). Prior to this, Benn had been banned for two one-day internationals for his part in an on-field altercation with Mitchell Johnson and Brad Haddin during the Perth Test in December 2009.

After his altercation with Benn, a fired-up Steyn quickly scotched any notions of a West Indian fightback with a three-wicket burst that accounted for D.M. Richards and Narsingh Deonarine in successive deliveries and Gayle four overs later. Shiv, in his accustomed role on a sinking ship, supplied an unbeaten four-hour 71, but Botha again ripped through the middle, and only Shiv's seventh-wicket partnership of 53 with Shillingford carried the contest into a fourth day. On the final day, Roach's hostility, which brought him three wickets, enlivened South Africa's short victory chase-but it also boiled over in his ugly mid-pitch confrontation with Kallis".

It is interesting to note a comparison in batting performances between both teams. On the South African team, some players averaged 61 plus; the highest average was 165.50. Set against these statistics, the West Indies four frontline batsmen registered between 31.8 and 75.00 on averages. Shiv was outstanding with a 300 run aggregate at an average of 75.00. This was followed by DJ Bravo's 33.20,

Narsingh Deonarine's 32.00 and Chris Gayle's 31.80. The figures are expressive of a disastrous batting performance. Here again, Shiv withstood the onslaught but the task was beyond him since all he could count on was the lower order.

In the last two months of 2010, the visit to Sri Lanka was inconsequential due to excessive rainfall which made the series impossible. There was nothing noteworthy about this tour (save for Gayle's monumented 333 and Sangakkara's century) when the Sri Lankan Cricket Board cancelled further matches with the consent of the West Indies Cricket Board.

Chapter 17

Dull Encounters

Shiv's relish for Indian bowling

As the years progressed, the problems facing West Indian cricket were manifold. In 2011, the player - Board feuding became more intense. The Board exerted autonomy, and defied soft political interventions by Caricom Governments. WIPA (West Indian Players Association) also had a strained relationship with the Board as some players expressed dissatisfaction in their dealings with the Board.

The failure in the World Cup in 2011 brought deeper agony. Senior players Chris Gayle, Ramnaresh Sarwan and Shiv Chanderpaul were excluded from the ODIs versus Pakistan in the April/May 2011. Gayle was omitted due to his conflict with the coach, Otis Gibson, but he had also defected to the Indian IPL cricket. Sarwan was furious when he was not called up to play in Guyana's T20 series and Shiv resisted when he was asked to retire. Here there was a misunderstanding as it was retirement only from ODI games as the Board felt he could not be fit at 40 for the 2015 World Cup. It was indeed absurd to request his retirement, particularly as he was performing in the ODI's. The method used lacked logic and was an indictment on a good player's performance. It would have been more sensible to exclude him from selection if his form was not good. This issue met with displeasure from his Guyanese compatriots, and the then Guyanese President, Bharrat Jagdeo displayed his anger by placarding with the sign "WICB is a disgrace" in the stadium during the last ODI match. The selectors were prepared to prepare younger talent for the next World Cup. Shiv countered by stating that his performance in the 2011 World Cup was hampered by the selectors' interference in his approach to batting. He contended that given his freedom, he would have fared better.

Amidst the turmoil, and in light of the treatment to Shiv, Tony Cozier described the confrontation as an "uncivil war". Against this background, cricket to the West Indian public was becoming more and more unattractive. There was crushing criticism and cynicism aimed at players and the West Indies Cricket Board.

In the midst of the turmoil, Pakistan arrived to contest an ODIs T20 and Test Series in May 2011. The entire series turned out to be a tour of dull encounters. West Indies lacked the presence of Gayle, Sarwan was unproductive and Shiv was ruled out of the second Test through shoulder injury.

Newcomers were given the opportunity to prove their worth but they disappointed. The series concluded with a 3-2 ODI Pakistan victory, a 1-0 West Indian T20 victory and a drawn 1-1 in the Test series. On the whole, West Indian batting lacked depth but the bowling armoury showed sparks that brought victory in the first Test. It was a much needed victory that gave some diehards hope.

In the first innings of the first Test at the Providence Ground in Guyana, West Indies' slender total of 226 seemed reasonable compared with Pakistan's meagre 160.

West Indies needed a sound second innings score to ensure victory. This seemed an uphill task until a partnership of 48 between Shiv (36) and Bishoo (24) allowed West Indies to set a target of 219. Thereafter, the pace bowling of Roach and Rampaul together with Sammy's decisive spell brought victory to the West Indies.

Test 1 W.I	**226**	**Pak**	**160**	**W.I won**
	152		**178**	
Test 2 Pak	**272**	**W.I**	**223**	**Pak won**
	377/6		**230**	

The second Test was played at Basseterre, St. Kitts, on a wicket which was relished by the Pakistan spinners – hard, dry encouraging turn and bounce. The Pakistan team showed resolve in their effort to triumph and West Indies did not take advantage of their early dominance.

The batting display was unconvincing in both innings; it was never enough to earn victory. A Pakistan innings of 272 was met with a 223 response from the West Indies. Pakistan's second innings performance gave them great advantage. This was gained through two centuries in the innings. Set a target of 427 for victory, the West Indian response of 230 fell dismally below the target. Sarwan's failure and Shiv's omission through shoulder injury made it easier for Pakistan.

Tony Cozier lamented the West Indian "diffidence" which permeated the second innings.

On the heels of the Pakistan tour to the Caribbean in June/ July 2011, India presented themselves in the Caribbean for a contest of three Test matches, in June-July 2011, five One Day Internationals and one T20 match. Shorn of the experienced Tendulkar, Zaheer Khan and Yuvraj Singh, India still asserted their superiority in their thrust to victory. The West Indies were "still struggling to transcend their only status". India won the T20, were victorious in the one Days and won the first Test at Sabina Park, Jamaica. They could have had success but for weather conditions and their complacency in the last Test.

Test 1 India	**246**	**W.I**	**173 India won**
	252		**262**
Test 2 India	**201**	**W.I**	**190 Match drawn**
	269/6		**202/7**
Test 3 W.I	**204**	**India**	**347 Match drawn**
	322		**94/3**

Shiv averaged 48.20 (1st placed) 1/100

In the West Indian team, the loss of Chris Gayle, and Sarwan's lack of form paved the way to an easier passage for India. Once again, following the Pakistan series, the West Indies fledging batsmen made no significant impression. The batting scores in the three Tests were - 173, 262, 190, 202 204 and 322. Only once did they exceed 300 and that was due to centuries by the debutant KA Edwards (110) and Shiv (116 n/o)

India too were not prolific with the bat and only climbed the 300 marker once. While India's batting was bolstered by Rahul Dravid, VVS Laxman and Suresh Raina, West Indies depended on Shiv, in his usual rescuing role. The centuries by K.A Edwards and Shiv ignited the innings in their attempt to repair the ruins of the front-line batsmen. Fidel Edwards' bowling was also the key factor in the drawn outcome of the last Test.

Of lesser account were disappointing scores from Adrian Barath and DM Bravo. Altogether it was another disappointing West Indian performance.

The statistics at the end of the series registered three batsmen achieving an average of 30 + - Shiv 48.20, DM Bravo 34.16 and Marlon Samuel 32.00. In contrast, there were Dravid's 56.2, Laxman's 48.6 and Raina's 46.4. Their averages were not phenomenal but enough against West Indies run-drought.

In the first Test, the now established pattern in West Indian performance was again revealed. As against Pakistan earlier in the year, West Indies were unable to sustain early dominance against the opposing team. After an impressive start which left India 'floundering' at 85 for 6 wickets down, the West Indies bowling outfit could not capitalize and they allowed one partnership between Harbhajan Singh and Suresh Raina to reverse their fortune. India were able to register 246. The response was disappointing as West Indies struggled to 173 with scores from Adrian Barath (64), Shiv (23) and Baugh (27).

After India's second innings of 252, West Indies were set a task of 326 for victory. The efforts of Barath (38), Simmons (27), DM Bravo (41), Rampaul (34), Sammy (25), Bishoo (26) and Shiv (30) fell short as no batsman devopled an innings around which the team total could be built on a wicket that posed no danger. Shiv's dismissal had also made a difference.

The second Test in Barbados was drawn but it would seem that the rain conspired on more than four sessions to deny India a second victory. Dhoni's sporting and challenging declaration, setting West Indies 280 in 77 overs on the last day almost paid dividends for his team. With dim light as evening wore on with a tense atmosphere on the ground, West Indies held on with 202 for 7 in 71.3 overs.

Some would describe as deja-vu the opening session of the third Test when West Indies claimed 4 wickets for 38 runs but then lost command. The discipline and application to press home an advantage has been a problem that persists in West Indian cricket performance. They had reduced India to 38 for 4 with all front line batsmen denied freedom to score freely. Then two of India's stalwarts, Laxman and Raina were allowed to revive their team with a 117 partnership in twenty-eight overs. This laid the foundation for their eventual victory.

In response to the 280 required for a West Indies victory, only Baugh and DM Bravo mounted an attack but this proved inconsequential at the end. The ever reliable Shiv was sluggish in his response in both innings, scoring only 37 and 12. The conclusion seemed a fair outcome.

Roseau, Dominica was the home of the third Test. West Indies first innings 204 was met with 347 response for India. To the West Indies' credit, there were two batsmen, KA

Edwards with a debutant's score of 110 and Shiv with 116 not out whose response in the second innings had reduced India's first innings lead of 142. It was Shiv's 133rd Test appearance and Edwards' impressive debut appearance. Both batsmen had embarked on a rearguard action, adding 161 to give the host some semblance of safety. Edwards showed strength in the leg side while Shiv denied India's intrusion and in the process achieved his 23rd Test century. In facing 343 deliveries, the one blemish was a dropped chance when on 25. His innings lasted eight hours and twenty -one minutes. Shiv also partnered Fidel Edwards in a 222-ball stand. It was the most deliveries faced by a West Indian ninth wicket partnership in Test cricket. Edwards accumulated 30, his career best to that date. Shiv remained unbeaten on 116. Though he laboured in his achievement, his innings was crucial to the team's fortune. It was Shiv's 133rd Test appearance and he had gone beyond being West Indies' most capped player, Courtney Walsh. ESPN Cricinfo comments: "Shiv was under immense pressure ahead of the final Test but came through with yet another fighting knock of real substance".

In response to Shiv's defiance, Ishant Sharma exclaimed: "Chanderapul is the most irritating batsman to bowl to." His comment is reminiscent of Shane Warne's earlier comment about his obduracy.

In Shiv's stay at the crease with Fidel Edwards, he guided Fidel throughout his innings. Their partnership brought energy to the West Indies crowd. Everyone was elated as Shiv "leaned, lunged, pressed back, tucked, tapped and nudged" in his defiance of the Indians. "With the departure of all others, he stood alone" were the words of Cricinfo writer Sriram Veera. Another Cricinfo writer, Siddharta Talya commented on Shiv's evergreen reliability: "As the wickets were falling. Shiv blocked out one end completely. He saw off the seamers with ease, driving and chipping them away for runs and displaying solid defence and farming the strike when Fidel Edwards joined him."

A draw spanned critical indignation from the Indian media. They were caustic in their treatment of Dhoni had not tried too hard to force a victory in this Test. In response to a target of 180 for victory in 47 overs, India got to the point of needing only 80 runs in 15 overs with 7 wickets in hand. To the astonishment of many, both spectators and critics, Dhoni abandoned pursuit of victory and seemed content with a 1-0 series victory. India, at that point, had Laxman and Dravid in the wicket. Dhoni, Harbhajan and Kohli were yet to make their appearance.

The question arose – Was Dhoni not convinced of his team's competence or capability or was it mere complacency? To the media, his decision revealed a lack of resolve or indifference to the game's sporting character.

Before their visit to India, West Indies won 1-0 in a two match contest vs Bangladesh in October 2011. But this was inconsequential. On their visit to India in the latter part of 2011 (Nov/Dec), the issue of West Indian early dominance (as demonstrated in the previous series with Pakistan and then India) became a matter of grave concern. Their inability on so many occasions to gain success from "promising positions squandered at a despairing rate" was Dileep Premachandran's comment on West Indian frailty. The visit to India, Premachandran says "encapsulated that feeling". It was also evident in the ODI series.

Test 1 W.I	**304**	**I**	**India**	**209**	**India won**
	180			**276/5**	
Test 2 India	**631/7**		**W.I**	**153**	**India won**
				463	
Test 3 W.I	**590**		**India**	**482**	**Match drawn**
	134			**242/9**	

Shiv averaged 54.00 (2nd placed) 1/100

In the first Test in Delhi the West Indian first innings of 304 was countered by a meagre 209 India response. West Indies led by 95 runs but a less than mediocre score of 180 in their second innings denied them any semblance of victory.

With a lead of 95, West Indies did not assert dominance. A disastrous second innings collapse (63 for 6) was agonizing. There were times when their spirit looked spent and was likened to "a lazy yawning drone" with no purpose and it was very possible that with a singleness of purpose they would have been "well borne without defeat". Once again Shiv resisted; he played cautiously but with a spirit of aggression. At 47 an lbw decision thwarted his efforts. His teammates, with the exception of Sammy, all withered in the storm. The target of 276 was met with five wickets to spare. A 1-0 lead was an obstacle to West Indian hope of early ascendancy.

Shiv's relish for competition with the Indians was demonstrated through his century on the first day. Wisden reports on Shiv's score of 118: "he was anything but stodgy as he picked off pace and spin alike. He drove beautifully and at times played the ball impossibly late." It was his 24th century and his seventh against India.

Sidharth Monga reports: "Chanderpaul drew support from a man who was two years old when he began the using bail to mark his guard in Tests. Kraigg Brathwaite, who became only the second West Indian player to score two fifties before his 19th birthday, has similar reserves of patience, idolizes Chanderpaul, and uses the bail to mark his guard. For 37 overs and 108 runs today, the youngest and the oldest member of the side did all that together, except that the youngest played the old-fashioned watchful innings and Chanderpaul turned the momentum with quick runs."

The statistics revealed that this was Shiv's 7th century against India. Now he was joint 2nd on the list with the most centuries against India. Gary Sobers and Viv Richards had achieved their 8th centuries. At this particular time he had equalized Viv Richard's 24th century. Only Brian Lara (34th centuries) and Gary Sobers (24th centuries) were at the top of the list.

A second Test defeat sealed the West Indian fate at Eden Gardens, Kolkata. It was an occasion of dynamic and dominant batting prowess coupled with clever spin bowling that demoralized the opponents. Any team that has to counter an imposing total is usually at a disadvantage. A mammoth 631 for 7 declared, confident and convincing from India's batting talent seemed to have dulled the West Indian spirit. Their response indicated how demoralized they were. Every batsman including Shiv and the promising DM Bravo failed in a 153 response. Shiv's failure at times was indicative of the strain on him by the frequency of West Indies collapse, although on many occasions he had come to the rescue in order to add respectability to the team's reputation. There were occasions when the stress would have been beyond him. He also felt depressed when his efforts were thwarted.

It took a second innings compulsive urge to try to redress the balance and salvage some measure of respectability. A total of 463 was achieved in an effort that was still uncompetitive. However great the effort, West Indies could not make India bat a second time. There was some good scores – Barath 62, KA Edwards 60, Shiv 47, DM Bravo 136, Samuels 84 and Sammy 32 but a collapse was disastrous and defeat inevitable.

West Indies' good batting in the first innings of the last Test at Wankhede Stadium, Mumbai, continued and on this occasion they accumulated a healthy first innings score of 590. India, however, battled to measure up to the West Indian target. They fell short by 108 runs but West Indies did not capitalize on the advantage with a low second innings 134. In this match Shiv did not play.

It was a match that had its exciting moments in the last three sessions and concluded dramatically as a drawn Test. Of significance was the absence of an injured Shiv. In Dilip Premachandran's words: "It was strangely reassuring for the tourists that the best results – the thrilling draw in

Mumbai, which finished with the scores level – came in a game he missed through a calf-muscle injury." At that point some delightful sparks of batting seemed burgeoning but only future matches would tell of the batsmen's strength of character and talent.

At the end of the series, a little comfort for the West Indians was their ability to score in excess of 300 on three occasions out of six at the crease. In terms of batting averages only DM Bravo's 67.33 and Shiv's (2 Tests) 54.00 were of significance.

A full year of cricket in 2011 with the World Cup tournament and tours with Pakistan, India and Bangladesh further revealed West Indian vulnerability.

Chapter 18

Patriotic Fervour

"When I go out to bat, I know I have to do a job for my team and the people of the West Indies."

Shiv Chanderpaul

The Australian tour to the Caribbean in early 2012 was described as the most competitive between both teams since the year 2000. The consensus among the cognoscenti revealed a series very well-matched though at the Test level West Indies faltered, giving the Australians the advantage. The outcome meant that Australia had retained the Frank Worrell Trophy they held since 1994-95.

In the current debacle, the West Indies were coming close to victory but found it eluding them. A key turning point was day four of the opening Test at Kensington Oval, Barbados. West Indies had amassed a handsome 449 total but it came mainly after the top order had gone for 240. From this point it was the tail-enders who rallied with Shiv to produce a respectable score. Shiv's innings was described as 'a mixture of deflection and dynamism'. In the process he earned his 25th Test century, a score of 103 not out.

Test 1	**W.I**	**449**	**Aus**	**406/9**	**Aus won**
	148			**192/7**	
Test 2	**Aus**	**311**	**W.I**	**257**	**Match drawn**

	160/8		**53/2**	
Test 3 Aus	**328**	**W.I**	**218**	**Aus won**
	259		**294**	

Shiv averaged 85.60 (1st placed) 1/100 3/50s

Australia's response was certainly not dynamic but rather a struggle as the top order batsmen found it difficult to score fluently against the pace of Fidel Edwards and Kemar Roach. Australia were 250 for 7 in response to West Indies 449, left only with the wicket keeper and the tail enders – the bowlers, Ryan Harris, Ben Hilfenhaus and Nathan Lyon. Shockingly, or perhaps not, over the next 150 minutes they amassed 121 runs and reversed the outcome of the match and series. Once more the 'predictable' occurred as the West Indies again could not dictate the course of the match. It was the ideal opportunity to take charge of the match. To allow the tail to wag freely was a great indictment to West Indian strength of will and stamina.

The risk-taking captain, Michael Clarke declared 43 runs behind the now demoralized West Indies team, and in quick time the West Indies were 17 for 4 and eventually 148 all out. Australia were ultimately victorious despite the rapid descending shade of night. It was another occasion when West Indian fragility was most apparent. A match which could have very possibly determined the outcome of the series had been surrendered through lack of initiative and application to the task at hand.

Heavy showers led to a draw at the Queen's Park Oval,

Port of Spain, in the second Test. The noteworthy parts from a West Indian perspective on the match were Kemar Roach's success as he claimed 10 wickets and Chanderpaul's steady partnership with Deonarine which appeared to be consequential but was blemished by Lyon's spin attack. His spin decimated the team's performance. In this innings, Shiv was denied his second century of the series when he was trapped LBW by Lyon's spin.

History began to repeat itself in Dominica where the third Test was played. Although on the first day Australia were in dire straits at 169 for 7, Wade, who came as a substitute, racked up a crucial 103 and was then joined by Mitchell Starc. They pushed up the score to 328. The West Indies, as a result, seemed to cave in.

The series has been described as one in which batsmen on both teams were ineffective against bowling on slow pitches. It was only Shiv who demonstrated consistency and an appropriate approach in the situation in which he was thrust. His scores were 103, 94, 68 and 69 in three Tests. Australia's top order did not rise beyond the 30 in averages. There were only four half centuries and not a single century. The West Indies line-up was similar in performance but the middle order (4-7) were superior in performance. The series record shows it was one of the lowest scoring ones in the West Indies in recent years.

In the series, Shiv played with grit and determination as he had so often done before. On a pitch unfriendly to batsmen, he tried to stave off defeat but was defeated in an attempt to dispatch Michael Clarke's bowling. His aggregate of 346 was more than any person in either team. In Dominica he exceeded 10,000 runs and was elevated to No.1 in the ICC batting ranking. Shiv was the second West Indian player after Brian Lara to achieve the 10,000 milestone and the 10th batsman in Test cricket to achieve it.

"I felt delighted as any other player will feel on such an achievement. It meant I was among a group of outstanding batsmen in the world. It was a great achievement for West Indian cricket. I had contributed to West Indies cricket and that was most important for me," he refelcted.

Both Shiv and DM Bravo with great resolve had been together at the crease in an attempt to challenge the 320 target and Bravo has high praise for Shiv's role in West Indies cricket. Bravo intimated that the Caribbean team's progress was influenced largely by Shiv's impact on the younger players: "The good thing about it is whenever you talk to Shiv and ask for advice, he's 100% willing each and every time to share his advice. We're very fortunate to have him in this team at this point in time and we enjoy his company; he's going to be around for a long time still. He's scored lots of runs and as young batsmen in the team we should try to take a page from Shiv's book as much as possible. Shiv's a guy who will bat first at training then be the last to leave the nets. So it's something for us as young batsmen to look at. The way he goes about an innings is special; he plays the ball on its merits and his concentration level is very good."

Bravo's comments certainly ring a bell with the praise showered on Shiv when David Warner achieved his 335 not out triple century feat.

Warner remarked that he had learnt a lot from Shiv while

playing county cricket with him at Durham. From Shiv he had learnt the art of batting through the day: "I learned this from Chanderpaul when we were at Durham. He batted on the bowling pitch for six hours." I said, "This is ridiculous, how can you do this? Chanderpaul said, If you're going to bat for six hours in a game you might as well practise it."

Shiv had achieved the No. 1 ranking in July 2008. ESPN reports that he held the No.1 for seven months. He briefly dropped to No.2 in February 2009 but returned to the top spot three Tests later after the final Test against England in Trinidad. In May 2009, he lost his spot to Pakistan's batsman Younis Khan. Shiv's rating then slipped as low as No.15 before he made his way back.

In response in an interview he exclaimed: "It feels good to be back in top spot in Test cricket. I am batting well at the moment, and when things are going well for you at the crease you try to keep going and building and look to make the most of every innings you play."

The character of the man and player is revealed through these words" When I go to bat, I know I have to do a job for my team and the people of the West Indies. Test cricket is the ultimate form of the game and this is where you want to perform and give your best. I will keep striving for more."

In the true spirit of the game he gave encouraging words to his fellow team mates although in the middle of a batting crisis. "You want to see young players coming through. Now we are seeing some of it and look towards the future. We have to plan that way."

Shiv's revelations and his performance in the game, his sense of identity and patriotic fervour surely would have made Michael Manley proud as it has with the likes of Hilary Beckles, Tony Fraser and Rudi Webster among others who have striven to preserve all that is uniquely national in our culture.

It is worthy to relate the encomium expressed by the Australian coach Mickey Arthur who had first seen Shiv in the 1998-99 West Indies tour of South Africa.

"Shiv's been outstanding all series. He's been quite brilliant really. He's certainly thwarted our bowlers. He's shown why he's got 10,000 runs in Test cricket," Arthur said. "Very uncomplicated technique even though it looks very weird on the eye. He's been outstanding – to get this right at the end of the day has just lifted our dressing room hugely.

I first saw him when he was very young. He toured South Africa and he looked a very, very good player then. In my last series that I had with South Africa as coach against the West Indies, I think Shiv got a hundred in every first innings so he was on track. In this series he got a hundred in Barbados, 94 in Trinidad and runs again here. I've just seen so much of him and can't help but admire the application and the desire to keep scoring runs. You've got to marvel at that – a fantastic achievement."

When the West Indian team members entered England for the Investec Series in May of 2012, they were nearly unnoticed since they had faded too far from the limelight. The side had been vastly depleted due to the lure of the Indian Premier League. Not present in the Test series were stalwarts like Chris Gayle – still at loggerheads with the West Indies Cricket Board – and all-rounder Dwayne Bravo. The "greener-pastures-seekers" were back in full force for the limited overs games which followed the three Tests but they did not perform, as was expected. Their team did not manage to win an international match in any format.

Test 1	**W.I**	**243**	**Eng**	**398**	**Eng won**
		345		**193/5**	
Test 2	**W.I**	**370**	**Eng**	**428**	**Eng won**
		165		**111/1**	
Test 3	**W.I**	**426**	**Eng**	**221/5**	**Match drawn**

Shiv averaged 78.33 (2nd placed) 2/50s

During the Tests, the West Indies proved inferior to the English team. The English captain reasserted himself by scoring centuries at Lord's and Trent Bridge. The West Indies under Darren Sammy's desirable leadership acquitted themselves admirably, which came as a bit of a surprise. As it happened, their great efforts were regrettably interspersed with unfortunate events.

Expectations were better in the One-Day Internationals, more so in the single Twenty 20 game, the format which complemented their style. Disappointment replaced high hopes and their only win was when they humiliated Middlesex in a 50 overs warm up at Lord's.

In the first Test at Lord's in May 2012. England won by 5 wickets. Lords has not usually been very kind to a visiting team in May. England had been rendered stronger by the return to form of Strauss who made his twentieth Test century. West Indies never found enough form to oust England of their supremacy. However, in both innings, Shiv made a statement with his total of 178 and gave England a bit of the scare.

Wisden comments:

"If you dig deeper you would discover a stubborn disposition in the West Indies performance. Maybe that says more about Shiv's for-the-long-haul approach in Test batting than anything else. If he had moved more aggressively, he could have been the first visiting batsman since George Headley (in 1939) to depart from Lord's having scored a century in both innings. In the first innings, he unfortunately ran out of partners when he reached 87 runs. In the second innings he was short of a century by 9 runs when he was l.b.w. while trying a sweeping stroke off a delivery by Swann.

Looking good wasn't important, but on day four, when he and the fully-recovered Samuels were putting on 157 for the fifth wicket to convert a loss into victory, Shiv's prowess was pronounced. Again, West Indies' fighting-back moments were eroded by their short comings, most patently the top-order two run-outs (one in either innings), and the quite careless strokes that ended two promising performances from Barath, the young Trinidadian batsman."

Strauss supplied the most meaningful innings of the series. He confessed that the monkey came off his back when he copped his first century since the start of the 2010-2011 ashes. When he reached 95, Strauss was dropped off a no ball from Fidel Edwards; but a redeeming cut off through backward point finished off the job.

From 259 for 3 overnight, England slid a little on the third day as the West Indies settled into an orderly off-stump line. Swann's attacking 30 in 25 balls brought the lead past 150; and the loss of 3 West Indian wickets for no runs in 9 balls just prior to tea tipped the balance severely. Broad barely ousted Strauss for the match award. His takings were the best for any bowler at Lord's since Botham got 11 for 140 against New Zealand in 1978. After having difficulty with his length, by the time the first innings finished, he had all systems on go again, grabbing 6 wickets in his final 50 deliveries for a Test best of 7 for 72.

Despite playing catch-up all along, the West Indies played with great determination. Trott went early to Roach on the last morning. When Peterson bottom-edged a pull off Gabriel, the West Indies garnered great illusions about prevailing but Cook's cunning and Bell's excellence brought them back to reality.

Shiv's record shows 87 not out, first innings and 91 in the second innings. It was unfortunate that he did not achieve centuries in both innings as he thoroughly deserved such a feat.

In the second Test at Nottingham, England won by 9 wickets. Trent Bridge was a serene sight, with a sell-out crowd really captivated by the sun's rays. Anderson played a major part in the four early wickets. The pitch offered so little assistance that Anderson decided to be a seam bowler instead of using his usual outswingers.

Bravo drove at Anderson's inaugural ball from round the wicket much to his great chagrin. Then Shiv was a happy warrior when the next ball, a well-directed bumper sailed off his armguard and found its merry way over the cordon. He had fought to win his third consecutive 50 when he played to Swann and got trapped on the back pad. He made 46.

Sammy slashed his way to 100, his second at first-class level. With well-formed forearms he heaved balls beyond the boundary. This gave his team a sporting chance. By the time he finally fell to the leg-side trap early on the second day, he and Samuels had put on 204, a seventh-wicket record at this venue.

Many folks took it for granted that if the West Indies could make 370, England could make thrice that amount. It wasn't going to be a walk in the park. Cook's uncertain action outside the off-stump caused him to edge Rampaul. Strauss was dominant and had passed three figures by the close but was only able to put on an additional 39 runs. The West Indies were having their ups and downs and when the damage descended on the third evening, it seemed as though they were heading for disaster. As Kirk Edwards was indisposed, Shiv was called upon to fill the number four position but he made a mistake and hooked a lifting ball bowled by Broad which got into fine leg's eager hands. But Shiv said it was not a mistake. He has played a loose shot in disgust in retaliation for the treatment meted out to him by the selectors.

Despite Bresnan's dubious inclusion in the team he became

a match winner. He advanced England's position when his subtly-contrived reverse swing disturbed the West Indian batsmen. Edwards had no choice but to find himself at the wicket to face Bresnan at 61 for 5 with eight balls of the third day yet unplayed. Edwards was not quite prepared for what anguish would be apportioned to him; in no time he was sadly retracing his steps with an unacceptable first-class tour average of 2.85. The West Indies would require divine intervention to emerge from their sustained stay in the doldrums.

Before the third Test in Birmingham in June, Shiv said, "I was working out at the gym and I felt a tear in my stomach above the right leg. I could not move while I was in the bathroom next morning but I had to go to the grounds for the usual morning warm-up practice. There I could not move my leg well. So I was sent for a scan which showed nothing. Then I was criticized by the selectors and coach to apologize to the team. Why should I apologize? Why would I not want to play Test cricket as this was the only opportunity I had to play? I looked forward to the Test matches because they were few. It was a case where the selectors were trying to discourage me. I say this openly and no one can deny this."

The Birmingham Test ended in a draw. The first day of this Test was dominated by rain and then more rain but on the fourth morning, Tino Best kept things from floundering. His was a super-performance. He made a surprising 95, the highest by a Test number eleven.

Strauss won the toss and after a brief while, Onions removed Barath lbw. It took some time but England's seamers would slowly pick up steam in the fray, (led by Bresnan) but just as he had done at Trent Bridge, Samuels managed the bowling masterfully - as he clobbered for six and four in two consecutive deliveries, pointing his bat at Onions as part of his ongoing banter. He finally got out at 76 off Bresnan. The end of the innings appeared imminent when Rampaul was caught behind off the third ball on the following morning.

West Indies 'enjoyed some measure of comfort' against New Zealand in the middle of 2012 and then later in Bangladesh. The West Indies established control over New Zealand from the start. Even when New Zealand began the Tests and One Day series with some promise they failed to follow through. They were caught somewhere between calamity and catastrophe.

The West Indies were rendered stronger because of the return of Chris Gayle who had settled his disaffection with the Board. He made a corking 85 not out and 53 in the Twenty20 matches. He celebrated his first international showing in his native Kingston after three years with 63 not out and 125 in two 50-over matches there. He then accumulated 150 and an unbeaten 64 to secure victory at North Sound in the Antigua Test, his first since the end of 2010.

That the off-spinner, Sunil Narine, was in a position to play for an entire tour for the first time was most important. Despite a relatively poor performance in England, he was now as stunning in the shorter formats as he had been in the IPL, taking 7 wickets for 46 in the eight Twenty 20 overs, and 13 wickets at a thrifty rate of 2.92 in the One-

Day Internationals. He had to toil a bit more in the Tests but was still quite menacing.

Test 1 NZ	**351**	**W.I**	**522**	**W.I won**
	272		**102/**	
Test 2 N.Z	**260**	**W.I**	**209**	**W.I won**
	154		**206/5**	

Marlon Samuels kept up his top form which he had flaunted in the Tests in England and slammed a couple of centuries before his home crowd at Sabina Park in Jamaica. His 123 out of 209 in the second Test was rather remarkable. This was followed by a tense fifty-two when the West Indies were struggling to reach a score of 206.

Kemar Roach, a speed and demolition merchant, was Man of the Series for taking 12 Test wickets. When Narine was not up to mark in Jamaica, Narsingh Deonarine rose to the occasion. In the batting department he and his left-handed compatriot, Asad Fudadin, also rose to the occasion in the absence of an injured Daren Bravo and with Shiv not finding sufficient form. Kieran Powell, aged 22, followed behind Chris Gayle with his first Test century, in an opening partnership in Antigua.

Shiv's contribution in this series was below expectations; it seemed there was a temporary loss of form with scores of 0, 9 and 43 not out In the first Test his first ball dismissal was a rarity- only his 6th in 244 Test innings.

West Indies staged a 2-0 victory – 9 wickets and 5 wickets

in both Tests – to bring some joy to the West Indian public.

In late November 2012, Bangladesh entered the series having had no exposure to Test matches for just under a year. The West Indies had taken part in eight in 2012. Yet Bangladesh at Mirpur surpassed the West Indies' score of 527 by posting an impressive 556, but they fared abysmally on the last day.

Test 1	**W.I**	**527/4**	**Bang**	**556**	**W.I won**
		273		**167**	
Test 2	**Bang**	**387**	**W.I**	**648/9**	**W.I won**
		287		**30/0**	

Shiv averaged 118.00 Man of the Series 1/203 not out and 1/153 not out.

The West Indies, after Gayle's pyrotechnics, went back to a more conventional modus. They had accumulated 527 for four before declaring. After the well-prepared Powell produced his second Test hundred, Shiv forged his twenty-sixth and stretched it to a second with a score of 203 not out taking almost eight hours. He had an unbroken 203 not out with Ramdin, who made his third Test hundred.

The second Test, at Khulna, resulted in a resounding West Indian victory. Their response to Bangladesh 387, a good Test score, was a colossal 648 achieved through the centuries of DM Bravo (127) Marlon Samuels (260) and Shiv (150 not out). It was difficult for Bangladesh to recover and the match concluded with a 10-wicket victory.

Shiv had entered after a healthy score was posted and this meant he had the freedom to take advantage without being circumspect. He departed undefeated having achieved his 27th Test century.

Shiv recalls: “In this second Test when I was 150 not out against Bangladesh the captain declared the innings. I was 13 runs short of 1000 Test runs in a calendar year. I was not given the chance to achieve it though we had all the time in the match.”

Chapter 19

Season of Despair

Loss of soul – Hilary McD Beckles

As the years progressed through 2012 the decline continued, although the then President of the West Indies Cricket Board, Dave Cameron, presented a positive picture of the status of West Indies cricket. In spite of the challenges to West Indian cricket, Cameron noted "some significant successes" and positive (strides). He pointed to the four Test victories, triumph in the World T20 and new Tv deals.

However, Tony Cozier in his response on the status of West Indies cricket as described by Cameron, was critical of his optimism as 'fantasy'. "It carried a touch of fantasy," Cozier affirmed. For Cozier, it was a season of despair. To give credence to Cozier's critical comment, West Indies captain, Darren Sammy's dejection was evident: "We cannot continue like this." This comment was the lament after four disastrous performances vs India and New Zealand. This was a crisis but its immensity was denied by the Board's administration.

Cozier continued to pronounce that performance was disappointing. It was only Shiv, the lone anchor, who continued to "shore up the fragile batting". He was on his 150th Test appearance, the first West Indian to achieve this feat.

To survive in a sport for such length of time in terms of years and Test appearances is a feat achieved by few sportsmen. It also indicates a level of success that earns a player such longevity. Peter Roebuck's admiration for Shiv was affirmed by this longevity in the game and his achievements which had revealed his versatility as a batsman. He would have continued to play much more, until his career was curtailed by the Board and selectors.

West Indies began the year in March 2013 with consecutive successes vs Zimbabwe at Kensington Oval, Barbados – (3 ODI, 2 T20) and two Tests – a 'sub-standard' team. Even so, in both Tests there were periods of West Indian fragility at 157 for 6 in the first Test and 114 for 3 in the second but Zimbabwe were unable to take advantage of the initiative. The only other bright spark in performance was Gayle's 101 and Shiv's 108 in the second Test at Roseau, Dominica. There were no other centuries. It was Shiv's third hundred in four Tests.

Test 1 Zim	**211**	**W.I**	**307**	**W.I won**
	107		**12/1**	
Test 2 Zim	**175**	**W.I**	**381/8**	**W.I won**
	141			

Shiv 1/100

The series in India which followed in November 2013 was described as more of a 'pilgrimage'. Its aim was to honour Tendulkar who was leaving the cricketing arena. On his indication of retirement, the Indian Board responded by creating a series to honour him with two Tests, culminating in a celebration of his 200 Test appearances. And though there were expectations of a century in his last innings, he departed gracefully with his score at 74. The series was disastrous for West Indies; it was a 2-0 Test victory in India's favour and a 2-1 India's victory in the ODI's.

In the first Test at Eden Gardens, Kolkata, after a modest West Indian score of 234, the spin of Shillingford destroyed the Indian upper order (85-3) but this could not be sustained as Rohit Sharma and Ashwin turned the tables with a 280 partnership in 72 overs. It was historic. At that time it was the third highest seventh wicket partnership and India's second highest against the West Indies. Previously, Sunil Gavaskar and Dilip Vengsarkar had accumulated an unbroken 344 partnership against Alvin Kallicharran's Packer reduced team in 1978-79. India were allowed to amass 453 but West Indies' second innings efforts were futile. The Test concluded with India's victory by an innings and 51 runs. The lone survivor Shiv, could not hold back the Indian team as he ran out of partners. The other players showed no courage in strength to buffer the variety of India's bowling armoury.

Test 1	**W.I**	**234**	**India**	**453**	**India won**
		168			
Test 2	**W.I**	**182**	**India**	**495**	**India won**
		187			

In the second Test at Wankhede Stadium, Mumbai, India won by an innings and 126 runs. It was another disastrous display by the West Indians. Within three days the match was completed – a humiliating performance in both innings. This was Shiv's 150th Test appearance, all forgotten in the adulation poured on Tendulkar's 200 Test matches. Again, Shiv played with grit but could not enhance his team's image on this occasion. He was dismissed on 41.

The visit to New Zealand in December of 2013 was a different experience as the new team was making its first appearance with only two of the established players, Shiv and Ramdin. The rest of the team were in India. Not surprisingly, this team was outdone by the New Zealand pace attack. It was a series best forgotten with all the woes the West Indies experienced. Their fast bowling never made any impression; Shillingford was suspended for "illegal action"; Sammy went lame and Rampaul had a finger injury.

The only bright spots in the series were Darren Bravo's maiden double Test century and Shiv's century. In the first Test at Dunedin, (University Oval) New Zealand, it was only Shiv who showed the ability to counter the New Zealand's attack by scoring 76 out of 87 deliveries. In the third Test at Hamilton, Shiv scored his 29th century and in the process surpassed Allan Border's 11,174 and becoming the sixth highest scorer in Test Cricket. However, it was a New Zealand 2-0 victory.

Test 1	**NZ**	**609/9**	**W.I**	**213**	**Match drawn**
		79/4		**507**	
Test 2	**NZ**	**441**	**W.I**	**193**	**NZ won**
				175	

Test 3	**W.I**	**367**	**NZ**	**349**	**NZ won**
		103		**124/2**	

Shiv av. 64.00 (2nd placed) 1/100 1/50

It was not the best of years for the West Indies. Their five ODI defeats by Australia, their elimination from the Champion Trophy, their distressing tours of India and New Zealand were too humiliating to bear both by critics and supporters.

Beckles, hurt and dejected as if his passion were spent but still in a rational state of mind and sound intellect uttered the words "loss of soul" in his criticism of the West Indian players. He hit at the heart of West Indian cricket disintegration - continued defeats, humiliation, lack of loyalty, lethargy, lack of courage and misplaced talent all divorced from the glorious age. Explicit in his saddened mood was his recognition of the fallen empire on a disastrous path.

Chapter 20

A Great Test Career Ends

Shiv's decline amidst the ruins

As the years progressed, the decline continued and was further exacerbated by the crisis between players and administration. Though the Board enthused that 2014 promised to be "a most exciting year for West Indies cricket," Tony Cozier, ever watchful, described the situation as one of "extraordinary decline of the game in the Caribbean".

Conflict between the WICB and players over financial arrangements climaxed in the cancellation of the tour although the cricketers were in India. The players were at odds with their association (WIPA) which had agreed to the financial terms without the players' consent. The Indian Cricket Board were incensed by this cancellation and held the WICB responsible for a 41 million loss (reported) incurred. An investigation into this crisis found the three parties, WICB, WIPA and the players all culpable.

Shiv's problems with the selectors were ongoing, particularly in the last years when he was achieving with consistency. He admitted he did not wish to recall the injustices meted out to him by some selectors and the coaches during these last years. It is interesting to note his views/opinions/statements on his role during the last three years before he was axed from the last team. First it was the shorter version of the game and then the Test matches.

Shiv recalls the events of the West Indies tour to India in 2014 for the T20, ODIs and three Test matches. The matches were called off during the shorter version of the game. He was in Guyana preparing for his visit to India to play the Test matches.

There was the persistent conflict among the WIPA, WICB and players and this was affecting play in India. It was reported that the Indian Cricket Board intervened with the hope of appeasing the West Indians but to no avail. In their obdurate stance the West Indians called off the tour. Shiv also commented that it was rumoured from a very reliable source from the team that some players and selectors did not favour his journey to India for the Test matches. He viewed this as a distraction from his intent to continue his Test Career, noting there were those who did not want him to eclipse Brian's record of 11,953 Test runs.

With the impasse still ongoing, the West Indies Cricket Board selected a team for South Africa. With all the numerous goings-on within the team there was a buzz. The Governments (through Ralph Gonzalez) tried to resolve the impasse but the agreement fell through because the Board unilaterally breached the terms of the agreement. This resulted in a crisis between Governments and the Board. Tony Cozier described it as the regional intergovernmental grouping in one corner, and the head Board in the other. It was a case of an irresistible force against an immovable object. It led to Ralph Gonzalez's, (Prime Minister of St. Vincent and the Grenadines), accusation against the

Board, "as a travesty of justice...... that reeks of vengeance, discrimination and victimisation". The impasse together with the players' recalcitrance only served to intensify the discord. The general disenchantment was evident in the poor attendances at the matches.

During this time, Shiv, the unwavering determined spirit, began to fluctuate in his performance. In 2014 vs New Zealand in the West Indies in June 2014, his aggregate was 195 with 84 not out being his highest score. Even so, this was the third highest among the top order batting. His 48.75 average bettered Gayle, DM Bravo and Ramdin's achievements.

Test 1	**NZ**	**508**	**W.I**	**262**	**NZ won**
		156/8		**216**	
Test 2	**NZ**	**221**	**W.I**	**460**	**W.I won**
		331		**95/0**	
Test 3	**NZ**	**293**	**W.I**	**317**	**NZ won**
		331		**254**	

Shiv averaged 48.75 (3rd placed) 1/50

In the first Test Man of the Series, New Zealand played at Sabina Park, Jamaica, New Zealand won by 186 runs. Facing a 'daunting' total of 508, West Indian batting frailty was evident against New Zealand's bowling attack. Faced with a target of 402 towards victory, the West Indies caved in at 216. Shiv at 24, succumbed to an lbw decision and only Ramdin, Benn and Shillingford resisted, but to no avail.

However, West Indian resolve in Test two at Queen's Park Oval, Trinidad, resulted in victory by 10 wickets. It was commented that after five losses in six Tests, three of which were against New Zealand, West Indies were able to reverse the odds stacked against them by winning the second Test and levelling the series.

In the final Test, at Kensington Oval, Barbados, West Indies had themselves to blame by not taking advantage of the initiative gained as New Zealand were allowed to climb from 194 for 7 to 293. West Indies led by 24 but New Zealand's second innings yielded 331. This gave West Indies a reasonable total to negotiate in an attempt at victory. The top order failed and in his second attempt Shiv at 25 failed with a stumping exit. The lower order could not defy the bowling attack apart from some brief resistance. It was the first time in his 266 innings that Shiv exited through a stumping decision.

New Zealand took the series 2-1

The victory versus Bangladesh was no great consolation although the records show 3-0 ODI and 2-0 Tests conclusion in favour of the West Indies. In the first Test, at Arnos Vale, St. Vincent, September 2014, West Indies posted a 484 total mainly through Kraigg Brathwaite's double century and Shiv's 85 not out but it seemed a hard-earned conquest. There was need for more aggression and less laborious entertainment. A ten-wicket victory was the seventh versus Bangladesh in eleven Test encounters.

The second Test produced another West Indian victory at Gros Islet, St. Lucia September 2014 but the victory was not of 'fanfare' elation. In his 158 Tests, Shiv had achieved his 30th century – 101 not out after he had posted an unbeaten 85 in the first innings. Wisden comments: "Chanderpaul, more than 20 years after his debut, contributed a characteristic double of 84 and 101, both not out."

In this series, Shiv showed that at 40, age made no difference to his single-minded devotion. After making 183 in the warm-up game, he remained unbeaten in his three Test innings, which spanned 12 hours 23 minutes and 558 balls and brought him 270 runs.

Test 1	**W.I**	**484/7**	**Bang**	**182**	**W.I won**
		13/0		**314**	
Test 2	**W.I**	**380**	**Bang**	**161**	**W.I won**
		269/4		**192**	

Shiv averaged 270.00 1/100

A period of drought followed the series versus New Zealand and Bangladesh in the Test encounters with South Africa and England. Shiv experienced a bad trot with scores of 21, 4, 7, 9 and 50 vs South Africa.

Test 1 SA	**552/5**	**W.I**	**201**	**SA won**
			131	
Test 2 SA	**417/8**	**W.I**	**275/9**	**Match drawn**
Test 3 W.I	**329**	**SA**	**421**	**SA won**
	215		**124/2**	

Shiv averaged 18.20 1/50

Critics felt Shiv seemed to lack the energy and resourcefulness of former years. Against South Africa, his last score was 50 at the Centurium Park after some low scores. He seemed a shadow of the hero everyone knew. In this contest for the Vivian Richards Trophy, the West Indians seemed to lack a competitive spirit. The first Test defeat at the Centurium Park was inevitable. Rain was the determining factor in Test two but South Africa emerged victorious once more at Newlands. The humiliation was dispiriting. Shiv's lacklustre performance brought him 91 runs from 5 innings – a far cry from his accustomed dominance.

In the first Test South Africa's formidable total of 552 for 5 seemed to have blunted any positive response. Every member of the West Indian team failed with four batsmen not exceeding forty and the reliable Shiv exiting at 21. A 201 total was demoralizing and there was further embarrassment and agony as they succumbed at 131 in 42.3 overs. South Africa won by an innings and 220 runs – a depressingly sad story. Here again, Shiv failed with score of 4.

In the second Test, at Port Elizabeth, December 2014, three days were lost to rain. Shiv failed in his effort to counter South Africa's 417. Only Brathwaite's 106 and Samuel's 101 made any impression on a total of 275 for 9.

At Cape Town, January 2015 in the last Test, West Indies' effort to save the series was futile. After limiting South Africa to a lead of 92, Shiv was the teetering victim of a leg-side stumping for 9. In the second innings West Indies tried to make amends and build a total for South Africa to counter. Shiv and Samuels started a recovery but it was to no avail as Samuels held out at 74 and then Shiv exited through a run-out decision at 50. South Africa was given a 124 target and this they accomplished with the loss of two wickets.

In his written commentary on the series, Telford Vice may seem cynical but his view cannot be contested: "With each one-sided session, the question thundered louder: What is cricket going to do about West Indies? It's just that they have no hope of rediscovering their dominance.

It is that they seemed to have no hope of competing consistently, of playing as if they don't respect their history. Cricket in the Caribbean is like bull-fighting in Spain; a strong cultural artefact, endured and tolerated more than enjoyed and treasured."

In a three-match series in the Caribbean versus England in April/May 2015, West Indies made a recovery in the last Test to stave off a series defeat. The first Test at North

Sound, Antigua, was drawn but England secured the second at St. George's, Grenada by a nine-wicket victory. The third match at Kensington Oval, Barbados, was a low-scoring one but West Indies' bowling efforts in the innings reduced England to 123. The challenge to victory was 192 and this they achieved with the loss of 5 wickets.

Test 1	**Eng**	**399**	**W.I**	**295**	**Match drawn**
		333/7		**350/7**	
Test 2	**W.I**	**299**	**Eng**	**464**	**Eng won**
		307		**144/1**	
Test 3	**Eng**	**257**	**W.I**	**189**	**W.I won**
		123		**194/5**	

Shiv averaged 15.33

A poor series versus England for Shiv proved the end of his career. After his failure versus South Africa he gathered a mere 91; his last innings score was 0 and this turned out to be his last innings in his Test career.

The stress on him was mental and emotional and this continued into the Test vs South Africa and England. Shiv recalls: "In both countries I was almost isolated and treated as a perfect stranger. There were words thrown at me that I would be out soon. They were making my age a problem. I remember at one of the meetings in the latter part of my career the coach lashed out saying that some of us feel that we have the God given right to play forever.

With all the negativities against me I was uncomfortable, mentally and emotionally stressed and as a result my performance declined in both South Africa and England. I could not focus on my batting. As I did not perform well against these two countries, my role in the team was uncertain although I requested a last series against Australia.

It was also strange that Clive Llyod, the Chairman of the selectors who should have known I was in Barbados, called for me in Guyana to inform me of their decision to retire me. I could not understand that.

After my omission from the team to tour Australia, Mr. Dave Cameron, President of the West Indies Cricket Club made an attempt to re-install me in the team and directed Roland Holder to arrange for my ticket to Australia.

I got the support of Philo Wallace who felt that I should be given the opportunity to continue based on my career performance. Phil Simmons had agreed with this but after discussion at selection level he changed his position.

Subsequently to Cameron's initiative, the selectors met hurriedly and was against Cameron's decision stating that younger players had to be given a chance. Another call from Cameron advised me of the last decision of the selectors. Cameron in his good attitude felt that players should be treated with dignity on leaving the game. It was considerate of Cameron to advise me on what was happening.

There were forces that were trying to get rid of me

because Brian's record was being challenged but it was not deliberate on my part, I needed 86 to reach Brian. This attitude and behaviour of the selectors was so distressing for me to lift my Test profile.

There were ugly remarks made by one of the selectors as reported by a liaison officer. One of the comments was 'there are many ways to skin a cat and this cat can be skinned'. With these negatives I could not focus. There were names of players called as replacement for me. All attempts I made for a last series were denied.

It must be noted that I was the eight player at the time to have scored 10,000 runs in the history of the game. The West Indies selectors should have been proud of me.

At the end of my career I got no great recognition for my services to West Indian cricket except the Vice Chancellor's match a benefit for me (I was unavailable but my son, Brandon, represented me). The Dominican Prime Minister was gracious in making me honorary citizen and the University of the West Indies awarded me an honorary doctorate."

The next West Indian assignment was Australia but the Board felt that Shiv's powers were waning and decided he was no longer eligible for the demands of Test cricket. Though he was in disagreement and requested a last Test encounter with Australia, he was denied by the Board. It is curious to note that he was a mere 86 runs behind Brian Lara's record of West Indian's highest aggregate but the pursuit of the record was not as consequential as his desire to play one more series for his pride and self-esteem. He seemed to yearn to exit his career with some positive cricket for himself and his audience but that request was denied. He also thought that he had merited inclusion in the series based on his distinguished service to West Indies cricket. It was one of the few times he departed from his reticence and stood up vocally for his cause. The decision to exclude him sparked of a controversy amongst critics and fans.

Chapter 21

Chanderpaul's Retirement

"I shall not be pushed into retirement."

Shiv Chanderpaul

It seemed evident to the selectors that Shiv's powers of concentration and consistency were declining with the failures experienced in the last two tour encounters with South Africa and England. It was surmised that age was the main factor which impeded his accustomed ability to stay the course and be the lynchpin in his team. To the selectors he seemed a shadow of the herculean image he had carved as a major sheet anchor in the team and, as Cozier describes him, as the 'defiant defender.' The prodigious years seemed at an end. On his bad trot he had scored 21, 4, 7, 9, 50, 46, 13, 1, 7, 25, 0.

Questions raised dwelt on loss of form or loss of the technical skills to combat bowlers. Was it a temporary lapse and could he have resurfaced if given another chance? Not-withstanding, the selectors felt his days in the sun were fading and there was need for a rebuilding of the team with the main focus on youth achievement. As a result, he was asked to relieve himself of selection so that younger players be given the opportunity to create a new image for West Indian cricket through effective training and development of attitude.

Contrary to the selectors claim of inserting young players,

there was already a group of young players in the team. For this reason, Shiv thought his inclusion was significant to contribute to the morale and support of the younger players in their endeavours as he had been doing with his contemporaries in the last decade.

There was serious debate on Shiv's exclusion from the West Indian cricket team. Some saw it as clinical treatment meted out to Shiv. There are those who on moral high ground, saw this rejection as an affront to his dignity as a player who had served the West Indian Cricket Board and the spectating public with great loyalty and dedication. Those who rallied for him are a "lot" whose minds and hearts were truly impassioned by the quality of his career, one which had impacted more in deeds than in words.

How do we reconcile the opposing views of the passionate seekers of justice and those who felt justified in excluding him in preference to the fledgling talent aspiring to revitalize West Indian cricket?

The arguments are passionate as well as rational. There is passion in those who rally for his inclusion but this passion is fused with strong rational thought. There is also the rationale explaining his non-inclusion based on his recent failures, the presumption that his skills were flawed and on the enthusiasm and anxiety to rebuild a competitive West Indian team.

Are the arguments flawed? There are no clinical or exact answers but reasons for public debate are justified.

Do you discard a player of Shiv's stature and achievements – one who has done yeoman service to cricket in its darkest years by denying him at least two matches as his swan song? This was all that he truly wished.

Is the lack of form (let's forget age) in two series strong justification for rejection? Tendulkar comes to mind. Sachin's failure in nine Test innings, a paltry 153 runs produced in nine innings and a 14-month drought which produced no centuries, were followed by a dramatic resurgence against the powerful titan, Australia. The allusion here may cause debate for the skeptics but it is good fodder for all to contemplate, whether it be Shiv, Sachin or Lara. Some will say this comparison is not justified because Tendulkar was younger so there was no need to axe him.

Further pertinent questions arise: Was there some moral obligation to allow Shiv the opportunity for some measure of success at the "presumed" end of his career after his failures in the last two series? Should he have been given the chance to aspire to Lara's milestone record, however trivial this may seem? After all, aspiring to milestones or great achievements in life is within the purview of each man's ambition. Such achievements demonstrate not only personal fulfillment but tell of a person's capabilities.

Every cricket fan remembers Brian Lara's ascension when he tried to achieve and surpass Sir Gary Sobers 365 record. It was admirable of him to aspire to this feat and he was graciously complimented by a magnanimous Sir Gary who was proud of Brian's achievement. Sir Gary was present to congratulate Brian on his feat.

Wouldn't it have been exciting or fascinating for the spectating cricket fans to view Shiv's attempt to set a new record during this Australia tour, particularly at a time when skeptics had retired him? Historical data revealed leaked e-mail conversations before the West Indies home series against Australia in June 2015. Among them was Clive Lloyd's message to him that he would not be selected because of loss of form. This was followed by one from coach, Phil Simmons who also intimated to him, their intention. Some measure of friction followed as Shiv replied:

"My request to finish up with the Australia series is not asking too much. It gives me a chance to acknowledge my supporters at home and the possibility of WICB properly honouring me for my contribution to West Indian cricket. I shall not be pushed into retirement."

The predicament he faced on his omission was most dispiriting; it eclipsed the joy he had experienced during his successful career. It seemed that some officials did not consider his desire to restore his credibility at the end of his career and the hope of preserving the image that he had carved during his prolific years. He wanted the well-earned opportunity to show his mettle and felt the Australian tour could have reignited his form. Was it asking too much for one who had experienced the rigours of cricket with determination and success? To many it was an injustice to a patriot who had fought for his region's credibility. His mother country, Guyana, was perplexed by the Board's decision and registered its anger and protests. There were those in the cricketing fraternity who referred to Forbes Burnham's intervention to recall Clive Lloyd to the team after a drought in his performance. This measure had restored Lloyd's creditable future in cricket both as batsman and captain.

Shiv recalls that quite a number of West Indian players have not been treated with the accolades they deserved. He quotes Vivian Richards as a good example of a great player who was snubbed on relinquishing his captaincy. It is pertinent to record here what Richard's claimed in his book 'Hitting Across the Line':

"I decided then that I would relinquish the captaincy. I had definitely had enough. It was the right time to go. However, I did make myself available to tour. I did think that people would see that I still had a valuable contribution to make. Older, experienced players can still win matches – look at Ian Botham or Imran Khan.

So, when I learned that I wasn't to go to the World Cup, I was a little disturbed. I asked why? Why? I found out, in the end, that there was a group of people responsible for getting me out and it had little to do with cricket. I will not name names. They know who they are. I was very disappointed because, in the past, I had bent over backwards to help some of these people. They knew that. But they just couldn't show any loyalty.

It was hard to take. After all those years, to come across a lack of support."

Shiv's impasse did bear with it some measure of unease as he claims he was virtually forced to retire. Media reports on "Why Chanderpaul Retired' that his approval to play in the Masters League champion was based on his retirement. ESPN Cricinfo recalls his words, "I was given a No Objection Certificate by the West Indian Cricket Board with a clause in it that I retire on the 23rd January. If I didn't announce my retirement they would have taken it back" and on a note of disappointment he told the Caribbean Media Corporation "I wanted one last opportunity to play against Australia before signing off, but couldn't do anything about it. Just put that behind me. If a player like me is treated like that, then think of how the younger generation will be treated."

The drama took a different turn when the President of the Cricket Board, Dave Cameron, took a decision to reinstate Shiv for the Australian tour but this caused strife among some Board members and selectors and resulted in his non-inclusion.

In Mike Atherton's coverage of this friction which was developing, he viewed Simmons' response as sympathetic but was firm in his belief that in the context of the game at that point, Simmons was compelled to choose the best team. Neither longevity nor public opinion was the criteria for selection. Their wish was for Shiv to bow out gracefully, not to have him omitted from selection. He was eventually left out of the team which virtually meant the end of his Test career.

The argument for his inclusion as against his "forced" retirement will continue to be an issue that concludes in conflicting verdicts. It is compelling to hear the voices of the cognoscenti as well as the interested parties who have followed the sport with open eyes. At the heart of the discussion there was immediate protest among critics whose indignation was directed at the selectors and Board of Cricket. There were the defenders who felt that Shiv's career had petered out and it was at its nadir. In their opinion his departure was justified.

It is interesting to reflect on the arguments advanced and to view this issue with some great measure of objectivity. The picture which stood out was that of a man at the centre of controversy which originated in Shiv's protest against the selectors decision to axe him.

Mike Atherton, though impressed with Shiv's performance over the years, was sympathetic towards the selectors. Once they had made the decision to omit him they were duty-bound to leave him out. They were convinced of their decision and no other consideration should be given to change that decision.

His place must be based on merit. It is merit that deserves consideration, not public sympathy. Atherton asserts that a player's feeling of entitlement does not always dovetail with the selectors' responsibility of choosing the best team.

In response to Shiv's conflict with the selectors' decision, Phil Simmons, new head coach denied that Shiv was treated "shabbily". He said that Shiv did not fit into the best squad to face Australia and his omission did not mean he was shabbily treated. The selectors felt it was not appropriate to select him on the grounds that it would be a farewell series for him. Simmons said the selectors did not see it fitting to pick Shiv simply to offer him a farewell series. "He has had a long and illustrious career and we know he's done a lot for West Indies cricket but at the same time when we sit down to select a team, we sit down to select a team to win a game against Australia, and to play the two Tests in the series against Australia," Simmons told a media conference.

Simmons stated: "When we went through the process, he

didn't fit in. It's not about giving someone two Tests to finish their career, it's about picking the best team to play the next game."

Simmons, along with selection chief Clive Lloyd, defended Shiv's axing, contending the Guyanese left-hander's form had declined rapidly. In Lloyd's and Simmons' evaluation, he had fulfilled his role, served his time on cricket's unfolding stage but Shiv felt stranded with an unfinished task and had been left to fade into oblivion.

Batting icon Brian Lara expressed his unhappiness at the decision to omit Shiv as 'shameful' and called on the West Indian Cricket Board 'to give the left-handed Guyanese an honourary send-off by selecting him for the two - Test series against Australia. The report on Lara's criticism of the Cricket Board reads:

But Lara, who scored 11,953 Test runs, and Chanderpaul just 87 runs away from passing, said the decision was another example of the way WICB disrespects its players.

"This has nothing to do with numbers or averages. What are they saying that Chanderpaul was given the last 11 innings to get the desired number of runs to break a record?"

"This has absolutely nothing to do with runs or numbers. It has to do with respect and Chanderpaul has earned the right to say goodbye in an acceptable way. In fact, he should be allowed to do it in his own way." he added.

Lara commented on the treatment Sachin Tendulkar received when he was about to retire.

He asked: "What did they do? They organized a Test series in his honour and gave him a farewell in keeping with his contribution to the game."

Lara describes Chanderpaul as an extremely competitive individual for whom cricket was his life. "From Guyana in 1994 when he made his debut to his last Test innings he gave his heart to West Indies cricket and what do we do.....drop him and that's it," he noted.

Lara said it was time the WICB started respecting the contribution of its great players.

"The manner in which they deal with their players is despicable and should no longer be tolerated. When you look back to so many of our heroes and the manner in which they were dumped, it makes you shudder."

Lara called for Chanderpaul to be reinstated for the two Test matches against the Australians and the series be established as his final series.

"In that way, there will be no hostility and whether he makes a double century or a duck, it doesn't matter, it will be his farewell series and the entire cricketing world will know that," he added. Lara said he would be pleased to be at the grounds when Chanderpaul played his last innings.

"He deserves it. The WICB and the Caribbean owe it to Shiv to send him off with dignity and respect. He has earned it," added Lara.

Lara's reaction springs from a mistrust of the West Indies Cricket Board's attitude to players. It also has its origin in his personal fractured relationship over the years during his career. There were several instances of friction and conflict between players, particularly Lara, and the Board's management. He was angered by the treatment meted out to Chanderpaul. For him, the victim was his long-time partner, one who had stood with him for the better part of his career, and in particular, the historic moment of his unique achievement.

Lara's response was sympathetic based on Shiv's contribution to West Indian cricket for over two decades. It is his belief that such a contribution should not be overlooked, especially when the request was made for one short series. In Lara's mind, he sees the hard bone of professionalism denying the human spirit. No one can deny the remarkable contribution of one who on numerous occasions was a 'defiant defender' in his ability to demand some respect for his team. Though in decline, even uncertain, Lara thinks the occasion was appropriate for a show of appreciation either in an effort to team success or even Shiv's personal fulfillment. It is the symbol of recognition for his role that takes precedence.

In Essentially Sports of June 10, 2015 Shreshth Jain in the piece - Shivnarine Chanderpaul - a tragic end? commented that it was most surprising to see a man who had been the most consistent performer in West Indian team, being dropped before a series against such a strong opposition but later conceded that one could understand the selectors' decision (whether one means the universal or one individual – SJ is not clear). However, Jain had hoped Shiv would have been given a last chance based on his credentials.

But Jain asks – "Is it the right call?" From Jain's knowledge he states that most people disagreed, and many cricketers have come out in support of Chanderpaul. though he recognizes that Chanderpaul has his critics on his method of batting. Jain feels it is extremely painful to see the treatment meted out to such a legend in Caribbean and world cricket. He has played in 57 Test series; been the most consistent for two decades; only in 16 series has he averaged below 30 and 49 times not out.

The question was raised: Are the failures in two series (he scored 183 runs in 11 innings) enough to warrant an exclusion from the team especially when there was clearly no adequate replacement. "Though not endowed with natural talent," in describing Shiv, Jain in his objective analysis, remarks that Shiv had "battled for every run, fought against the odds and relished every crisis that came along with dogged determination."

What became more disconcerting was the performance of the newly-fledged talent which suffered heavy defeat at the hand of the Australians.

The issue of Shiv's selection brings to mind the cases of two modern day cricketers of India, Sunil Gavaskar and Sachin Tendulkar, who both had periods of batting drought but who were not deprived of opportunities to recoup and then contributed to their team's efforts and successes. In 1977, Gavaskar was experiencing a period of drought. In five innings, he seemed detached with scores of 0, 18, 39, 24 and 4 but then prospered, scoring one century in every three Tests. The other great, Sachin Tendulkar experienced a bad trot in nine innings but his selectors never lost faith. He then registered 241 not out against a strong Australian outfit and then went on to the historic 50 centuries. The nay-sayers would say there two players were younger than Shiv, so there was still cricket in their career.

Earl Best's piece on "Should Tiger tail wag West Indies cricket dog"? refers to the many who have made pronouncements on Shiv's retirement, acknowledging those who were very disturbed by Shiv's omission.

Earl Best goes on to cite the various experienced West Indian players who felt that Shiv was at the end of his career. Jeffrey Dujon, Michael Holding and Brian Davis, according to Best, all felt Shiv could "no longer command a place on the best team". It was Michael Findlay who, more open-mindedly, felt that Shiv's experience "might well prove useful, indispensable even, against the battle-hardened Aussies."

The arguments will never cease in bars, on street corners and sporting fields but the Earl Best commentary is a rambling piece of work in his analysis of the issue. It clearly shows a negative attitude to Shiv's performances, making reference to Shiv's batting stance and absurd comparisons with other West Indian greats.

How does he view Shiv's achievements in England after his retirement? Coupled with his negativity, though acknowledging his contribution somewhat, was there need for the irrelevant assertion that Shiv could never be among the greats? And how would Best view Shiv's achievements in England after his 'forced' retirement?

What is more enlightening was the aftermath when Shiv proved to be dominant in English League cricket in his performances and his mature contribution to the counties, particularly Lancashire.

The former President of WIPA, Dinanath Ramnarine expressed his dismay at the WICB's treatment of top players' departure from West Indies cricket. In Shiv's case he saw it as the disgraceful treatment of a great batsman. Guyana's former Minister of Sport, Dr. Rupert Roopnarine expressed the view that Shiv's departure had not been treated appropriately. To him such a gigantic contribution should have been dealt with appropriately. Roopnarine felt that though Shiv's form was questionable, he should have left the cricketing scene in a "dignified way".

It is significant to note that many critics of the sport expressed an interest in Shiv's omission. It would appear that apart from his record over the years he was well-loved by the spectating public all over the world as a sportsman with a demeanour that carried with it a sense of innocence, oblivious to the machinations around him except for rare occasions when he was supportive of his teammates in their challenges with the authorities.

The Times of India noted that during his long tenure, he had seen changes in players, coaches, Boards and the fluctuation of methods and rules. In the same vein of appreciation like that of Essential Sports Shreshth Jain, The India Times viewed Shiv's two decades in cricket as career-defining. "No player except Sachin Tendulkar had played more Test cricket than Shiv. That he retired only 87 runs behind Lara tells of his 'unflappability'." In paying tribute to Shiv, the Times affirmed:

"With his retirement, the fading strands connecting current cricket to the 90s have diminished significantly. Chanderpaul was one of the very few remnants of that era in which West Indies cricket started to fade quickly. He saw plenty, from being part of a team in decline to suffering some of West Indian cricket's worse defeats, to featuring in some rare wins in the past 15-odd years."

There was also the accustomed criticism of his batting stance, "but when the dust settles on Chanderpaul's career the worth of his runs will be judged with aura and appreciation." The Times reports that not only did he score consistently but it was his obduracy "in countering teams' momentum and psyches". This made him the thorn which provoked opposite teams and unsettled players.

Chapter 22

End of an Historic Career

Having constructed something upon which to rejoice

T. S. Eliot

There were several occasions when he was exhilarating, exuberant and also in mercurial moods.

Peter Roebuck

Amongst the batsmen who have played a significant role in West Indies cricket and also made a tremendous impact on the sport, Shiv stands out in an august company – a cadre of West Indian greats who have left an enduring legacy in cricket history. His place is secure and celebrated in the record books and among a cricketing public who remember him with affection and respect.

There are many greats who have traversed the field of play and among them he stands out with his accumulation of runs against all bowling attacks. This, he has demonstrated, while confronting pace and spin with confident resolve. Though noted for his defensive approach on many occasions, there were several occasions of aggression both in Test and ODIs without being impetuous. It must be noted particularly in the words of Albert Baldeo that "those who are critical of his doggedness fail to appreciate he was often the lone warrior in many lost causes at a time when West Indian cricket sank to unfathomable depths and responsibility forced him to eschew glamour and style for dependability, and audacity for attrition." In an analysis of Shiv's career, Aroon Naraynsingh, a past cricketer with immense knowledge about the game declared: "That there is need for a sheet anchor in a Test that is scheduled for five days. There is need for players with staying power or stamina to prolong, especially to defend, if there is need to stave off defeat. Shiv not only defended, though some would say he was obdurate but he also defied the attempts with aggression successfully on many occasions, either trying to save his team or capture victory."

In the same vein of thought, Ian McDonald asserted that in Test cricket, "occupying the crease is a vital factor in the game. And in that respect Chanderpaul stands on the Olympic cricket podium with Dravid and Kallis."

Tony Fraser expresses the view of Shiv's batting: "you displayed in your 'tiger-like' disposition your commitment to the West Indies cause".

Fraser further comments that Shiv showed "that he possessed the West Indian flair for the spectacular but preferred to use it judiciously. When in fluent mode, driving and placement rather than blasting of the cricket ball were a couple of the most notable features of Chanderpaul's batting and against all foes. In his turn at the crease Shiv Chanderpaul was a humble servant of West Indian cricket."

Two avid followers of Shiv's career, Vic Oditt and Pradeep Abdool, acknowledge that Shiv truly qualifies to be classified as an icon: "His long and successful tenure as an international cricketer has few, if any, in comparison. His frail stature, his unorthodox stance, his unselfish approach, his humility and his unassuming personality all combined to make him one of the most respected cricketers on and off the field. As Guyanese, we are proud that he was honoured to have an important street named after him. Young cricketers would do well to study the man himself and his exploits to try to emulate him."

While others slumped, Shiv was the essence of reliability; steadfast as he decimated the opposing attacks on several occasions at the crease. Many of his innings carried the burden of responsibility. For this reason his sheet anchor role may have seemed dogged on occasions. At times when he seemed indisposed to stroke-making his argument was very plausible as he had indicated that 'atlas-like', he had to patiently establish respectable totals for his team. Nor was he petrified by the attack that came to him as he displayed a supreme measure of confidence.

It is also evident that his role as sheet anchor in the middle order and his ability to adapt as an opener in the shorter version of the game made him a complete batsman. In his role as an accomplished batsman coupled with his modesty and devotion to the game, he had captured the imagination of a wide, international spectating public. Cricket was and is a religion to him.

Shiv's youthful years were confined to village cricket in Unity, his home. This he relished abundantly and this enthusiasm took him to Georgetown where his mettle was tested. There his resolve, determination and diligence did not go unnoticed. There were years were of sacrifice, commitment to the game and aspiration to be a good cricketer.

Shiv's early years in Test cricket revealed a person single-minded, facing the bold world of cricket – journeys to foreign lands, facing unfamiliar paths, living in and out of pavilions for the duration of matches whether he played or not. The experiences allowed his cricketing personality to flourish and mature as the years progressed.

Some critics have viewed him as a good player and many others have recognized him as a great, outstanding cricketer, but they all see him as one who made significant contributions throughout his career except for a few lean periods. The burden of bringing respectability to his team was thrust upon him on several occasions. In doing so he was untiring in his progress at the wicket as if his energy was inexhaustible; he was the veritable scourge of the best bowlers of his time as he prospered in the midst of pace and spin. He showed an emboldened approach in resisting defeat. Against the bowlers, his serious countenance was apparent as he knew they were after him since he resisted with firmness and concentration. Moreover, he had achieved some of his greatest triumphs in the face of defeat and his team's struggles.

Peter Roebuck another veteran cricket analyst, has captured faithfully the type of batsman we have seen in Shiv during his expansive career.

"Shivnarine Chanderpaul provides a notable counterpoint to the contemporary game. At once he is inimitable and timeless – he has scored runs yesterday and today and will tomorrow. Just that he goes about it in his own sweet and deceptively frail way, relying on deflections and glides - as opposed to power. In short, he is a reminder that, even now, cricket has many faces and talent can take many forms." This sums up succinctly the Shiv we know.

Roebuck envisages him as one who has "defied straight-forward conventional thought" but was also too modest to confront anything beyond his circumstances.

In Shiv we see a player with courage and resolve – a resolve to fashion his own batting style and he has been successful with this, away from all the orthodoxy which at times stultify creativity. But one must understand that Shiv was never trained in the conventional methods that coaches apply. And any comprehensive or incisive research of his career will tell of his successes and tremendous success against stalwarts, like England, Australia, India and South Africa on their home grounds.

Roebuck defines him as an excellent batsman, excellent because were it not so, he would not have lasted so long and achieved so much. There were several occasions when he was "exhilarating, exuberant and also in "mercurial moods". When in full flight he seemed to be spawning runs on the grassy turf.

Shiv's consistency has been remarkable. A comparison can be made with many who began with great success but who vanished from the scene with little fanfare. We can all remember the remnants of the fragile cricket life of many who faded through lack of passion and courage to persevere. The achievements during Shiv's two decades of play were done in adverse circumstances, either by saving his team from defeat or mitigating the extent of defeat. He appeared slow at times in particular, in his sheet anchor role, but also demonstrated the mercurial side that Roebuck recalls.

David Currie describes Shiv at the wicket when he made a century in 69 balls in 2003 against Australia. For Currie "Chanderpaul was awesome in attack." At that time it, was the third fastest century in Test cricket. Before this, Vivian Richards had led with a 57-balls century vs England and Jack Gregory of Australia had accomplished it in 67 balls vs South Africa in 1921. Shiv's record now stands at fifth place following Misbah-Ul-Haq (56 balls in 2014) and Adam Gilchrist's 57 ball century in 2006/2007. This century made greater impact as Shiv's visit at the crease was a rescue mission for his team which had been reduced to 47 for 4 and soon after Lara was unfortunately dismissed at 53 for 5.

It was an arduous task to change the fortunes for his team but with his daring and courage to defy the Australia attack, he accomplished the century with 15 fours and 2 sixes. The 69-ball achievement was an occasion for revelry. The sound of music accompanied by dance was expressive of the solidarity of a people yearning for a sport which brought enjoyment and merriment to gladden their lives. It tells of the powerful impact of sport, particularity cricket in Caribbean life.

In the same series, Shiv's century (104) was one of the main thrust, together with Sarwan's in a successful pursuit of Australia's formidable 418. Both Shiv (104) and Sarwan (105) brought life to the match, and a record performance in West Indian success.

There were performances worthy of recognition, such as his partnership with Lara during the latter's record breaking score, his first century vs India in 1997, his 203 not out off 370 deliveries vs South Africa in 2005 as captain. This innings included 23 fours. It was a match in which West Indies accumulated 543 for 5, and an innings which included Wavell Hind's 213 but South Africa's obduracy, technique and skill defied the West Indian attack to earn a draw.

Another memorable innings was his 149 not out off 136 deliveries vs India in a 2007 ODI match at Nagpur. Set a target of 339, it was only Gayle's 50 and Shiv's 149 not out which brought the West Indies 14 runs short of victory. It was an innings of "wristy strokeplay" but in a losing cause as he did not receive ample support from his teammates.

One of his memorable innings often described as the "510 ball and 675 minutes epic" was a score of 136 not out vs India in the fourth Test in Antigua in 2002. His performance earned West Indies a vital drawn Test. Eventually, in that series West Indies won the fifth Test and the series. Shiv had gone on to two more fifties.

There are the cognoscenti who would remember his 103 off 248 balls vs Australia in Barbados (2012), an innings of defiance though Australia won 2-0. Shiv's aggregate of 346 was impressive with scores of 103 not out, 12, 94, 68, 69. Of promising talent shown at the age of 21, was his score of 80 vs Australia in the 1996 World Cup tournament but West Indies "suffered a sensational collapse" to slip into a five-run defeat. In 2007 he scored 446 in three Tests at an average of 140 and his 86 runs in boundaries off 109 balls. These are just a few of the great achievements in his career. Indeed, one of the most cherished moments early in his career was his presence as partner in Lara's historic innings in Antigua in 1994. Shiv's support as a young lad was unwavering and determined.

It is significant to note the Guardian's (of London) salute to Shiv. "Chanderpaul was shaped, too, by the circumstances of his career which has exactly overlapped with the decline and fall of the West Indian team. Lara did too, but he was so richly blessed that he always seemed to rise above his teammates, a man apart. Shiv seemed to have spent his talent propping them up."

Lara went in 2006, Ambrose in 2000, Walsh in 2001, Richardson in 1995 and Haynes in 1994. Shiv had played with 100 others since he made his debut. And even the best of them – Chris Gayle and Ramnaresh Sarwan – have come and gone all 42 of the players in 5 Tests or fewer."

The Guardian continues: The final years of Chanderapul's career have too often been characterized by what Wisden called the 'yawning gap between his skill, commitment and experience' and that of his teammates. After Lara quit, Chanderpaul took the load. He's been carrying it ever since, always unbowed, often undefeated."

Over the years his maturity was revealed in his acceptance of his role in his team, showing the ability to confront difficulty, with strength of will and fortitude. He has made a statement to present cricketers and younger ambitious ones that the road to achievement lies in one's endurance, courage and a sense of purpose. His physical dexterity was fused with unflagging assiduity or marked absorption at the crease. His consistency against both types of bowling contributed to his eminence as a complete batsman both at

Test level and the ODI events.

Against diverse opponents in diverse conditions he was fully engrossed. The difficult challenges never daunted him nor "dried the sap out of his veins". In him his colleagues saw the rare ability to survive amidst adversity. It was a strong test of his character and will as he revealed the maturity to face the challenges presented.

To emerge beyond the complexity of a team's failure and constant feuding with the Board requires strength of character. Shiv said that the constant bickering was disturbing but he tried to focus on the game and tried to be oblivious of the continuing impasse. Amidst the turmoil and dissension and continuing failures, it took great resilience to meet the robust challenges from rivals.

Whether or not he is the unsung hero, his life is simple, modest, self–effacing and generous. These qualities endear him to a people whose affection for him is undisputed. He will remain heroic in his endeavours as he contributes to cricket in his retirement. Cricket is indeed richer for his superlative achievements as he has carved an indelible niche in the game's history.

In his retirement and contribution to cricket at County level in England, he was prolific and respected as an achiever. David Warner, a prolific scorer himself, pays tribute to him as a colleague at Durham.

Shiv's stints at county cricket were successful during his Test career and as well as his post-Test career. His years in county cricket were some of the best times he experienced. He got used to the conditions and felt at home playing for his different counties. There was something almost incomprehensible which attracted him in his English cricketing experience. His time at Durham, Warwickshire, Derbyshire and Lancashire were memorable times. He was in the company of players such as Ryan McLaren, Josh Butler, Stephen Croft, James Anderson, Steve Harmison, Michael Di Venutu and performed with skill and consistency. It was remarkable that his post-retirement achievements at County level demonstrated his ability to contribute to the game with distinction. A perusal of his record will real that he was still capable. So enamored of the sport, Shiv has gone on to claim his place by his involvement in professional coaching of cricketers.

"His achievements have been manifold, as player and in his recent duties as coach and as an ambassador of West Indies cricket," one report read.

In his cricketing career, Shiv exuded positives which have impacted on his performance. He impressed upon the cricketing world the essence of true passion and all loyalty to his mission. He embraced the collective spirit in guiding his younger colleagues with encouragement but was always inclined to defend them on the grounds of inexperience. Alertness of mind, singleness of purpose and resilience, all human attributes towards success – he revealed through example. His legacy is not only confined to centuries and records; it goes beyond to demonstrate the rich possibilities of loyalty to one's craft and his moral and cricketing support to his colleagues. In doing so, he has reaped the gratitude and appreciation of a multitude who have perceived him as one devoted to the game with passion.

In recognition of Shiv's achievements and service to Caribbean cricket, the University of the West Indies found it imperative to honour him with the Hononary Doctor of Laws (LLD) Honoris Causa of the University of the West Indies.

Postscript

As the century progressed to the millennium, West Indian cricket experienced a diminishing presence on the international scene. The most adulated and celebrated masters of the game for almost two decades were gradually dethroned from their Olympian heights. What a fall it has been!

In their ascendancy West Indian cricket appeared as a dynamic force, rivalling established teams. Victories were achieved with flourishes, a sense of romanticism in their approach to the game; their daring and audacious spirit as exemplars of both classical strokeplay and innovative, creative batsmanship were coupled with an arsenal that derailed the best batsmen.

Now in these times, Tony Fraser views the past and laments the present: We have forgotten and foregone our historical contributions to the game. Many amongst players and administrators are not aware of the seminal and outstanding contributions we have made to cricket, and the dominance exercised in periods of conquest.

Fraser continues: There is a serious deficiency in the make-up of our players/teams to triumphantly engage the extended battle and to grind our opponents into submission.

Fraser views our cricketers as players who can't sustain the momentum gained and are only capable of short bursts of performances. This has been seen many a time when our players have gained the initiative and cannot prevail with sustained effort and enterprise. It is a problem of discipline and passion to achieve with intensity.

Michael Manley viewed these victories as gained with 'good nature, with style, often with humour but with conclusive effectiveness'. Caribbean society shared a spirit of cohesiveness built under Worrell's tenure; a sense of nationalism pervaded and was reflected in the solidarity among spectators. Manley lamented the fall from grace.

The sixties to the nineties, save a few lean patches, was a period of summer's exuberance and vitality, of the glory of triumph and an unassailable presence among the cricketing countries as the cricketers soldiered on to almost unprecedented success in cricket history.

Since the early years there were all indications of a team 'coming of age', mature in execution and exulting in progress. Our islands can recall the exploits of Constantine, Martindale, Headley, Stollmeyer, Gomez, Ramadin, Valentine and the coming of Worrell, Weeks and Walcotts as a trio, moving to the era of Sobers, Gibbs, Charlie Davis, Derek Murray, then Kanhai, Bacchus, Lloyd, Richards – the fearsome four – pronged attack and the advent of Lara among a few others who have ascended to Test level with distinction. Lara's era saw a few accomplished players – Richardson, Bishop, Hooper, Walsh, Ambrose. The last link of reputable players after Lara's departure has been Shivnarine Chanderpaul who rallied on for two decades, during which he had the company of Gayle, Sarwan and Samuels. The early years paved a path for a tradition of progressive cricket, life-like, entertaining as well as triumphant in both sun and rain.

The years of Richardson, Lara, Ambrose, Walsh, Bishop,

Hooper, Adams and Chanderpaul were years of fluctuating fortunes but of gradual descent as decline beckoned. After Lara's departure, Shiv was the only link with the past and his role as batsman was restricted to sheet anchor to save the team's credibility as a Test playing nation. But there were also several occasions of his dynamism and of dynamic strokeplay with consistency. There was also longevity in his illustrious career.

The records reveal evidence of his sterling performances in both Test and ODIs – middle order batting and as an opener – innings which demonstrated his versatility. The description of a complete batsman has been defined by many critics who recognize one who can be comfortable with both fast pace and intriguing spin bowling. Shiv was at home with both. His 30 centuries and 11 ODIs centuries, a Test aggregate of 11, 867 with an average of 51.4 are a true testament to his status as a great batsman. He never wilted under pressure, never crossed with authorities until he was asked to retire. This was an incident which derailed his personal pride as he felt he could have had one more series to negate the failures of the last two. In the process he showed strength of character, a maturity over the years and a departure from the reticence he has been known for. He is now mature in thought and reasonable in speech, cautions but confident in his interactions. He has left a young squad of players, some with sparks of brilliance but yet to be nurtured into mature, successful players. As with Lara's departure, with Shiv's we still appear "a heap of broken images".

The perennial comments made from the days of Michael Manley, Hilary Beckles, Tony Fraser and Tony Cozier and others on the state of West Indies cricket and its growing crisis of failures are most relevant today – Every critic in the Caribbean discerns, in their outpourings on our demise, the negatives that have stultified success viz lack of self-discipline and self-motivation, constant feuding within the team and that almost indefinable lack of passion to create and construct valiantly. Rudy Webster asserts that those attributes create the energy that takes you nearer to your goal. He continues, very forcefully, that the depth of a player's self-motivation and self-discipline determines the level of success. It is the indomitable will which guides positive attitudes and actions.

Webster draws allusions to wars where soldiers must be motivated into battle and compares it with players on the cricket field. Players must be inspired to fight as victory is motivated by the will, spirit and mental toughness of the man who leads and the players who follow. This analogy brings to mind Henry V addressing his army at Agincourt as they prepared to battle France, and inspiring his yeomen to show the mettle of their pasture,

In fact, leadership must motivate not only in sports but also in worthy enterprises, and players must internalize their mission with passion and purpose. From Webster's experience with Australia, India and Sri Lanka and the West Indies he has concluded that in attitude, behaviour and performance West Indies current players can't compare with those of yesterday. "A willingness to learn, work ethic, self-discipline, self-motivation, self- awareness, self-reliance, hunger for success, commitment, fighting spirit, mental toughness, handling pressure, concentration and other mental skills," all contribute to success. A lack of these positives leads to decline and decadence.

Hilary Beckles complements this revelation with a treatise that stipulates reasons for the decline. In it he has outlined ten theories of decline but essentially emphasizes reasons which have impeded cricket progress in the West Indies. i.e disunity and divisiveness in regional unity, external forces that sought to diminish and disrespect its achievement, ineffective leadership, (visionless leadership) collapse of team solidarity, mismanagement at the administrative level, global commercial attraction such as IPL and T20's, but the most graphic and powerful statement that captures the imagination is Beckles' description which emphasizes how pathetic is our cricketing presence (or lack of it) in the Caribbean.

"Cricket fields in remote villages that once fostered the skills of youth are now abandoned and left to grazing sheep. Trees that provided shade for village critics of youth technique and methods are now meeting places for a smoke and a drink. The village academy is closed in most places; the plumbing is broken in the basement."

Beckles' statement tells of the abandonment of the game, lack of interest, opportunities lost and an erosion of all that was built before. The foundation had been shaken and new vistas for development limited.

Though critical of the status of our present circumstance, Hilary Beckles has always retained a positive outlook hoping for transformation.

The state of our cricket brings to mind, T.S. Eliot's 'What are the roots that clutch / what branches grow out of this stony rubbish?' It reflects the complex state of our cricketing culture in the 21st century. Eliot's comments are relevant, not only to 20th and 21st century decadence but appropriate to our circumstance. Stony rubbish tells of hopelessness, and the "rocks" he sees "without water" reflect the barren, sterile state of our cricket.

In light of these treatises, it is appropriate to conclude that Shiv Chanderapul's success was motivated since he was a little chap brought up in a cricket environment, learning of the cricketing heroes in Guyana and the Caribbean. The struggles he endured as an underprivileged youth inspired him to emulate the heroes he saw. It is through his passion and the deep desire to become someone of worth that Shiv, guided by familial ties, was able to emerge with an image that endures today and will for generations. One of the attributes later in his career was the intelligence to realize that he needed someone, i.e a manager, to help him exploit his ambition for greater success. This he did with the assistance of a manager, Chris Thakoorpersad, who instilled in him all the positives that make for success. Needless to say, if other players in the Caribbean had used this course of action, the road to success would be easier to attain. Cricket has gained and will gain if individuals of the calibre of Chris Thakoorpersad are engaged in mapping the road to one's success.

The role of individual guidance for youngsters is pertinent to engender self-motivation, discipline and a passion for success. Emphasis on practice at their game will certainly inspire cricket development in the Caribbean. Each young talent needs to internalize the wisdom to conquer, the maturity to sense the values of success and of the legacy he can leave after a fine career.

There are lessons we can all learn from Shiv and some other legends of the sport who have lived with that love and passionate desire to achieve, not only for their self-esteem but also because of their patriotic fervour and native loyalty to their team and country and region. With Shiv, it was love for the sport which inspired his perseverance and skill. It is one reason for his serious, combative spirit. It is that love which guides one's actions and determines one's attitudes. That love and impulse to achieve were well interwoven to produce abundantly.

Essays on Chanderpaul

TONY COZIER

Reliable yet misunderstood - 24th January 2016

Shivnarine Chanderpaul was the bedrock of the West Indies middle order over 20 years. But the circumstances leading to his inevitable retirement weren't pleasant.

It is typical of the present state of West Indies cricket that Shivnarine Chanderpaul's retirement from the game he mastered in his peculiar style for 21 years, over 164 Test and 268 ODI's, should have been inappropriately shrouded in controversy.

It was predicated by his omission from the home series against Australia last June. He was 40 then, and an average of 16.63 in his previous six Tests in South Africa and in the Caribbean against England, was a sign that the end was near. The selectors' decision showed no compassion.

The chairman of the panel, Clive Llyod, the legendary captain during West Indies' prolonged period of domination in the 1980s and a fellow Guyanese, wrote to advise Chanderpaul that they had "decided to move on with younger players for the future".

"You have been a great player for the West Indies and have given excellent service to the game and to West Indies supporters all over the world." Llyod added. "We hope that your skills will be utilized in the future and we wish you all the very best."

It was nothing less than a letter of termination, immediately and inevitably setting off enraged reaction. Unusually, cricket administrators found themselves on the same page as public opinion.

The Guyanese Cricket Board (GCB) charges that the selectors were "seeking to destroy" Chanderpaul. "Our Board just cannot believe nor fathom the thought process behind the wanton dropping of the most senior, reliable and dependable batsman of the West Indies for the 21 years," they said. "Is this the way the selectors intend to treat our esteemed cricketers after more that two decades of service to the people of West Indies cricket?"

West Indies Cricket Board president Dave Cameron pressed the selectors to reverse their position as the Board "needed to honour him". Even after Chanderpaul's exclusion from the squad against Australians was announced. Cameron arranged for him to fly from Guyana to Barbados to join the training camp, insisting that he should be picked. Much was made of the statistic that Chanderpaul, already West Indies' most capped Test player, needed just 46 to surpass Brian Lara's 11,912 runs as the leading run scorer we well, but Llyod and his people were not for turning.

Chanderpaul was never easily prised from the crease. Characteristically, he played on for Guyana. In the end, he missed the challenge of cricket at the highest level and accepted the unavoidable.

It will be an anguished wrench. Cricket has been his life.

He was little more than a toddler when his father, Khemraj, uncle and whoever around was available in his village of Unity on the outskirts of the Guyana capital, Georgetown, bowled to him, hour after hour, in a vain attempt dislodge him.

The first indication that West Indies' newest batsman had arrived was an unbeaten 203 in an Under-19 "Test" against England at Trent Bridge in the summer of 1993. A year later, he waddled to the wicket in outsized pads on his home ground of Bourda in Georgetown for the first of his 280 Test innings, against England. His selection, at 19, was as debatable then as was his eventual exclusion; his response was a defiant 62.

It immediately defined the character of his batting over the next two decades. What you saw was what you got. He was the antithesis of the stereotype of the dashing West Indian strokemaker. There was none of the left-handed flair of Lara or Garry Sobers or the muscular power Llyod or Chris Gayle. He simply did it in his understated way, earning most of his runs unshakeable patience allied to steely wrists and keen eye for profitable nudges and deflections through gaps in the field.

He took 510 balls and close to 11 hours to compile an unbeaten 136 against India in Antigua in 2002. In 2008, he roused himself from a numbing blow to the helmet to compete a hundred in Kingston against Australia.

It was not a say that his batting was entirely one-dimensional. He can lay claim to the joint fourth-fastest hundred in Test cricket, off 69 balls against Australia in Georgetown in 2003. His top ODI score of 150, against South

Africa in East London in 1999, required only 136 runs.

His several foibles immediately identified him at the crease, none more so than a stance that became so increasingly front-on it was generally described as 'crab-like". Whatever it was called, his record was proof of its success.

"When I started, I was very side-on but would work across the crease and struggle for balance," he exclaimed, confirming early video clip "I gradually began to open up as I found I could balance a little better." It didn't come easily. He spent hours in the nets practising the shot before he felt comfortable. It typified his determination and commitment.

But for an inevitable additional of a few ounces, he was still as slender at the end as he was at the beginning. He never took to the diamond studded earrings, gold necklace and designer sunglasses that became the standard fashion wear of the youngsters around him.

He briefly experienced the infighting that can undermine any sports team when he was made West Indies captain in 2005 after a strike by senior players. "It was a very difficult period for me," he recalled. "As captain, I wasn't getting any support. A lot of things were happening in the field. I'd come to the ground worrying how I was going to deal with these things and I couldn't focus on my own game." It prompted his resignation: Lara took over for his third stint in the post.

Ever a man of few words, his views on the game came across in quiet, measured tones. They were simple and invariably made sense, although not often heeded by the modern generation.

"If you play bad shots, you're going to get out," he once told me. "If you hit the ball in the air, you're going to get out. If you can bat to 50, can bat to 100." He proved the theory 30 times in Tests, another 11 in ODIs.

He saw the advent of T20 cricket as contributing to the decline in West Indies' batting standards. "guys just give themselves room in the version and fire, he said. "They don't care if they get out. That's why Test cricket will always be the ultimate. It tests you as to whether you're a man or a boy."

Although he sees plenty of natural talent among the batsman who will fill his spot in West Indies teams of the future, he detected little of discipline to go with it. "I see guys batting well and scoring, yet they still want to do something fancy," he said. "The pitches in the West Indies may not be the best, often up and own and two-paced, either seaming around or spinning, but that's when you should be fighting to surpass not giving away your wicket."

These are points he is trying to drill into those now coming along. Among them is his son, Tagenarine, Brandon to family, friends and fans who opened the batting for West Indies in the U-19 World Cup in 2014. Also a left-handed, he played alongside his father two seasons ago in the same Guyana team in West Indies' first-class tournament.

His might well be the next Chanderpaul on a senior West Indies scoresheet. If he follows half his father's mantras, he will be a significant addition.

Based on his 49 not-outs in Tests, selfishness is a tag sometimes attached to Chanderpaul senior. It was a charge that ignored both the effect of his position at No.6 in a team with a limp tail-end and the question of how much worse West Indies would have been without his reliability over an active span longer than any other.

Heavy defeats in their last seven Tests already verify how much he was missed.

Tony Cozier has written about and commented on cricket in the Caribbean and internationally for over 50 years.

Cricket was his Mariner's Compass

RAJGOPAL NIDAMBOOR

Cricket mirrors a sublime sense of beauty. This consists of the batsman on the TV screen, or in sight, for the most part. This is also 'received' through the 'ears' of the sound — of the bat stroking the ball by the skilful composition of mind and body mechanics, not to speak of the consonant proportion of resonances in the stadium.

There is a sense of delectable harmony too — when a batsman is on song, or 'in the zone.' You'd call it a higher beauty. Yet, the concept is largely relative — a batsman's talent, flourish, or grace, may appear beautiful to one person and the reverse of beauty to another. It is, therefore, best to reflect as to what most powerfully attracts the eyes of beholder and seizes the spectator with ecstatic delight — for if we can distil what this is, we may, perhaps, as philosopher Plotinus would have articulated, use it as a ladder that empowers us to ascend into the extent of beauty and review its vast expanse. This is one element.

Let's now delve into the other element. When psychologist Abraham Maslow studied the self-actualised individual, he arrived at the idea that such individuals are above the pack, or a cut above the rest. They are capable and adept in transcending the myriad stressors of life and achieving their utmost potential through peak experiences — in our context, on the cricket field.

Self-actualisation incorporates a veritable string of attributes — right from creativity, courage, humour and calmness to conviction. They are not just expressions of strength; they play the role of 'shock-absorbers' for that inevitable tempest, or the ups and downs, in one's career — aside from other vicissitudes. In contemporary thought, this element has a new expression — 'hardy personality.' You'd call it the extension of Maslow's 'model' that reflects three qualities: to dare, persevere and manage.

Shivnarine Chanderpaul exemplified such attributes — in a manner born. He was the quiet exemplar of what mind scientists evidence that a majority of us use, but a tiny part — about 3-4 per cent — of our inherent talents. Not our full, or actual, potential. Because, when we use them, at times, we not only surprise others, but also ourselves.

Chanderpaul was an outstanding example of that profound, well-organised, self-actualised, intensity-focused cricketer who worked endlessly on his true, if not natural, god-gifted potential, day-in and day-out, and took his game to a new level with his own description of beauty and guts. There was also something striking in his armour. His unconventional batting stance. It was unusual, yet beautiful — if only one went beyond the delineation of beauty, or its quintessential credo. Chanderpaul never ever dropped his guard. He was always there, unswervingly, with his passion for cricket — even at the 'forced twilight' of his remarkable career.

The philosopher Plato regarded virtue, courage and human fulfilment as being fundamental cogs to leading a productive career. He said that wisdom has much to do with the intellect just as much, or more, as a wise individual uses their mind to understand reality and applies them to their daily life. The 'mariner's compass' for the wise individual, as Plato put it, is often guided by rationality in the choices they make. In Chanderpaul's case, the mariner's compass, or radar, was his cricket bat. His sense of courage had also much to do with how he faced adversity. It was this essential trait that helped him to face and overcome difficulties, hardships, or 'selectorial' bias, including internal, or other conflicts, with pluck, poise, hope and refined grace, come what may. This was, in principle, the epitome of his innermost strength; also, resilience.

The philosopher Aristotle too believed that life, or career, for each of us, is keyed to a purpose and the function of one's life is, therefore, aligned to achieve that purpose — with more than a surplus element of empathetic steadfastness. Aristotle was convinced, no less, that the purpose of life, likewise, is related to 'worldly' happiness and thriving through the usage of reason and absorbing the best in everyday life — in Chanderpaul's case, on and off the cricket field. Aristotle believed that there was an unambiguous, crystal clear, connection too for such a description in every individual's life — focus, aim, or goal.

Put simply, Aristotle's sublime directive epitomises the fact that each of us, whatever our status, or situation, in life should use our capabilities to their completest potential to experience happiness and career satisfaction, also fulfilment, through regular 'mindful drills,' and not just application of our conscious, or realised, endowments and capacities. It is a given, as Aristotle put it, that human achievement is, as a rule, energised by purpose and independent action and that we should all take delight in being exceptional at what we do — whatever the framework of our talents. You'd certainly think of Chanderpaul as being West Indies cricket's spinning wheel, or pivot, in the context.

For a deeply religious, spiritual man Chanderpaul, who is also into regular meditative practice, defied every obstacle that came in the face of challenge. Yet, when he was robbed of his 'swansong,' he put up a brave countenance. He represented another paradigm too in that slagheap scenario. What is it that enables one to persevere in overcoming obstacles and setbacks that, otherwise, subjugate the less disciplined and less committed? Simple. Self-discipline. Here's why. When a self-disciplined guy like Chanderpaul, faced 'coerced difficulty,' he rose to the challenge and emerged stronger than ever before. Besides, he called upon his inner resources to find solutions to challenges. In so doing, he stood firm in his pursuit to which he was fully committed, in word and deed. Sadly, the powers-that-be were far too myopic — they, thanks to their skewed way of thinking, did not give him his due.

The prospect of overcoming odds with equanimity is not as easy as it may sound — more so, when a fairy tale has gone sour, albeit there is a certain paradox to it. Agreed that some of us are remarkably resilient — while others seem to throw in the towel, pronto, following a minor disappointment, or frustration. Chanderpaul was in a league of his own. He never ever lost his solid ground, also pleasant smile — a natural part of his psyche, also cricket 'gear.'

Chanderpaul always knew his capacity — the ability to bouncing back in the wake of a squall. There were more than a handful of such situations in his remarkable career. It was something that set the stage in enhancing his resilience and promoting self-recovery through positive thinking. We all know that Chanderpaul's great comebacks, be it cricket, or personal life, were fuelled by large doses of optimism and positive thinking, which also included positive 'walk-the-talk' with oneself — in the batting crease, or outside of it.

This was Chanderpaul's strength. It 'energised' his self-discipline — to think positively. His watchword was: 'Don't give up.' 'This too shall pass.' 'Success, or happiness, is just around the corner.' 'Keep trying,' etc., More than anything else, Chanderpaul visualised a positive conclusion. He never wasted time commiserating over an adverse event, or wallowed in self-pity.

"Resilient people," as Mihaly Csikszentmihalyi, PhD, the noted psychologist, observes, "are good at transforming chaos into order." Besides, they are able to take a seemingly hopeless situation and convert it into an activity they can manage and also relish. Chaos, it is evidenced, spurs them to new heights of imaginative problem solving. Chanderpaul celebrated the idea, thanks to his persistent self-discipline and focus. His self-discipline was just not related to discipline; it was a consistent ingredient that helped him to develop patience, which is yet again imperative for persistence. When one attains the two facets, they would be more than willing in investing as much time as necessary to achieving important self-governing attributes — just as Chanderpaul did when he was unceremoniously 'ousted' from international cricket.

This was, indeed, the cricketing key that enabled him to be optimistic — that there were other opportunities after his halcyon days on the field, especially in finding new avenues to doing better, or starting afresh in life. What's more, he was realistic too. He knew one thing from the inside out — that when the new initiatives one has envisaged fit neither the reality of the outside world, nor one's own internal realm, it's time they changed the trappings. Chanderpaul seems to have achieved that prospect — on his own terms.

There won't be another like him — what with his unusual, yet remarkable batting stance that empowered him to perceive what others did not, perhaps, 'see,' as it were — again.

Rajgopal Nidamboor is of Indian nationality. He is a wellness physician, writer, editor, independent researcher, columnist, author and pubisher.

Cricket Book: ***Cricket Boulevard***.

A Master Still at Work

IAN MCDONALD

I have been writing about Shivnarine Chanderpaul for more than twenty years, before he played Test cricket. And I have been watching him bat for longer than that, when he was a schoolboy in the old days when I used to go to the GCC regularly and often sat down with drink in hand to look at Club cricket. It was at one of those Club matches I remember, sitting next to one of Bourda's old stalwarts who might have been watching cricket there for fifty years, and seeing with him this frail schoolboy studiously and skillfully and staunchly playing out over after over from a couple of quite expert bowlers with assurance and time to spare, hearing the old man say, with an approving shake of the head, the prophetic words: 'See that one there – he going to make bowlers cry!' Yes, indeed!

Just past the age of 40 Chanderpaul has fashioned what must be now seen as one of the very great Test careers. An extraordinary aspect of this career is that he has steadily got better and better as he has got older. He has become in the years since 2007 a world master. In his career from 1994 to 2001 he played 49 Tests, made 2,833 runs and averaged 39.34. In the period 2001-2007 he played 52 Tests, scored 4,948 runs and averaged an astonishing 71.71. Very few, if any, have ever matured into such a marvellous fruition.

What is noteworthy, and perhaps unsuspected, is that Shiv Chanderpaul's strike rate has gone up in this latter period compared with how he started. In his first 49 Tests his strike rate was 40.56; since 2007, in 57 Tests, it is 44.11. It is a myth that Chanderpaul's scoring has got slower and slower. With rare and wonderful exceptions when he showed for all to see that he had the ability to score as quickly as any of the swashbuckling masters, he has always been a deliberate scorer of runs; he has always valued his wicket highly for the sake of his team and himself. He has always been fully aware of the great batsman's first rule – you don't score runs back in the pavilion. He has not got slower. He has simply got better and better until, with an average of nearly 72 in his last Tests, he must be numbered among the very greatest of batsmen who have ever played Test cricket.

The incomparable George Headley strode like an Atlas through West Indies cricket in his time, carrying a disproportionate share of the burden of their batting when he played. Chanderpaul, since the great and charismatic Lara's retirement, has played much the same role as Headley. Since Brian Lara's departure Chanderpaul has averaged over 70 while the rest of the West Indies top order has averaged 32, an astonishing statistic of one player's single-handed and single-minded dependability in a time of frailty. In this period Chanderpaul has averaged a century every 5.7 innings (and think of all those 50s) while the rest of the West Indies top order has averaged a century every 17.3 innings. An Atlas indeed!

One thing is sure, Chanderpaul must be numbered among the very top Test batsmen of all times in one important category. He values his wicket more than almost anyone has ever done. He is in the top five of the all-time list of those who have faced the most deliveries in Test cricket. Here is the list: Rahul Dravid – 31,258; Sachin Tendulkar – 29, 437; Jacques Kallis – 28, 903; Alan Border – 27,002; Chanderpaul – 26,710. And he is still playing so he may climb higher yet. The only batsman in the history of the game who has faced more deliveries per dismissal (with a minimum of 6,000 balls faced) is Rahul Dravid who averaged 123.06. Chanderapul is second with 122.04. Next on the list are Jacques Kallis – 120.46, Mark Richardson – 118.87 and Steve Waugh – 114.67. It is not a statistic often mentioned – never in the 'limited' world of non-Test cricket – but in Test cricket, where occupying the crease is a vital factor in the game; it is very important. And in that respect Chanderpaul stands on the Olympic Cricket podium with Dravid and Kallis.

Especially to those who have consigned Test cricket to history and swear that limited over cricket – and in particular the Twenty/20 variety – is what the game is all about. It may seem strange, but I love watching Chanderpaul bat. His cramped and peculiar front-on stance, his fidgety preparations ball after ball, his still schoolboyish figure standing steady at the crease when it matters fascinate me. His near-perfect judgement of what delivery to leave alone and what to play astonishes me. His application of when to nudge for one off the front foot, cut for two off the back foot, stroke for four through mid-off, mid-on or cover, pull for four or stoically and precisely defend I find unique. Why on earth should big hitting be thought preferable to or somehow more admirable than a well-executed single past point or a skilled defensive shot to a good delivery? Music does not have to be loud to be beautiful. An old, master's painting has its place, surely, even in an age of the comic strip.

I love Chanderpaul's batting. An almost fanatic follower of all sports, I am drawn to watch limited-over cricket – in the last few overs of close encounters. But I am drawn to watch Chanderpaul's batting any time and all the time he plays. For me he stands for something that should never be lost in the great game – superlative skill subtly wrought, patient application of deep knowledge of the game, perseverance through highs and lows, an artistry which does not need to lambaste to be successful, the spirit of the master craftsman and genius of his chosen trade.

Long may Chanderpaul continue! He has already secured his place in the pantheon of the very great Test batsmen; 158 matches, 11,684 runs scored with 30 centuries, 65 fifties and an average of 53.10. God of the far pavilions willing, there will be more to come. A master is still at work. He is looking remarkably fit and spry and quick in the field. He does not drop catches. He runs for that vital second run more eagerly then most. And I remember that the great Jack Hobbs after he was 40 years old scored 100 (or was it 98?) first-class centuries before he retired – including, we should note, a Test century scored when he was 46 years 82 days old!

Ian McDonald: Caribbean poet and novelist.

West Indian commentator, Reds Perreira, on

Shivnarine Chanderpaul's Test debut

I grew up in my native Guyana hearing and reading about fairytales, Jack and the Beanstalk and Snow White and the Seven Dwarves. But, a story on Shivnarine Chanderpaul is, no doubt, a very rare fairytale.

It all started twenty-one years earlier when he was born in the humble fishing village of Unity on the east coast of Demerara twenty one miles from Georgetown – and, coming from the Pomeroon River in the Essequibo I understand fully what is a humble life.

In his early years, his father and uncle and the extended family played a mighty role in developing his early skills and practice sessions were held on the beaches of Unity with the entire family taking turns to bowl to him, which, sometimes, went on for hours.

His development as a young lad was through whatever system existed then at Unity and east coast cricket, but Shiv was clear in his mind that, above all else in life, he wanted to become a cricketer.

His development as a batsman and the runs he put together were immediately noticed by the Guyana youth selectors making his way eventually into the under 17 and under 19 squads and then a West Indies Under 19 cap.

On their tour to England in 1993, he amassed 372 runs in

two Test matches with an average of 124 and impressed all with an innings of 203 at Trent Bridge batting in his own particular open stance, which he later made famous throughout the world.

Shiv made his first class debut for Guyana against the Leewards in 1992 scoring 0 and 90 with bowling figures of 7, 2, 24 and 0, whilst his second game that year was against a strong Barbados combination hitting 66 and 12 not out with figures of 9, 3, 26 & 0.

In the opening match of the 1993 West Indies season, he further picked up important batting experience playing five further matches whilst he was carefully looked after by the senior Guyana players, Hooper, Harper, Sarwan and Butts.

He scored 27 against the Windwards and took 1 for 21 and 1 for 24 with his legs spin. In the match to follow, he only scored 5 against the Leewards, but played a major role with the ball, picking up 4 for 48 form 16 overs and none for 60 from 23 overs.

He was, again, to meet a competitive Barbados attack and scored 35 and 56, but fell short in his next game against Trinidad & Tobago with only 13, bowling over 3 overs without success.

Against Jamaica, in the season final first class game, he only managed 31 and 48 after looking set to go much further.

The best, however, was yet to come for when selected for the West Indies President XI, he picked up his maiden first class century against Pakistan of 140 undefeated and taking 4 for 68 off 18.5 overs.

The season of the following year, no doubt, played an important role in him becoming a genuine all-rounder and his performances were as follows:

vs Jamaica – 41 and 34 and 1 for 60 off 15 overs

vs Windwards – 57 and 7 not out supported by important spells of 2 for 28 from 16 and 3 for 26 from 13 overs

vs Barbados – 1 not out in a rain affected game, but was impressive getting 3 for 32 from 21 overs, which included 8 maidens

vs Trinidad- 101 and 64 and from 16 overs, he took 2 for 22

vs Leewards – 11 and 73 and 2 for 63 from 14 overs

When England opposed Guyana on the 94 tour, he, no doubt, had a disappointing game scoring 3 and 28 bowling only 4 overs and finished 0 for 11.

His Selection

England had played their opening test in Jamaica with Desmond Hayes and Phil Simmonds occupying the opening role, with Simmonds failing in both innings at Sabina.

When the selection committee met in Georgetown, they took a decision for Captain Richie Richardson to replace Simmonds as Haynes' opening partner, which left a place in the middle order to be filled. My information is that Roland Holder was considered for this position, but the selectors made the surprise selection of Shiv Chanderpaul based on his all-round ability, both with bat and ball. The rest is history as he walked out to join Jimmy Adams in front of a record Bourda crowd, welcoming the 21 year old, whose pads and bat, at the time, seemed too large for him. And, the fairy tale was completed.

Disappointing Career Ending

In the ongoing series, there was no doubt that this great West Indies batsman was having a bad run and I felt that the chairman of the selectors and coach should have met with Shiv before the start of what turned out to be his final Test match to say that we have every confidence in your ability to come good, but your future may depend on how well you perform in the upcoming Test.

Without the required success, he was allowed to leave Barbados without further hearing from the West Indies management thought lack of communication. Later when he returned to Guyana efforts were made to reach him by phone, which seemed all too late. It was a sad end to a great contributor to West Indies cricket.

Appendix 1

Here is a report by the Express 27th October 2018 on the occasion of Shiv's UWI honour.

All for the West Indies – Chanderpaul says UWI honour ranks with on-field exploits.

Looking back at his two decades of hard work and sacrifice in the service of West Indies cricket, legend Shivnarine Chanderpaul, who was bestowed with the Honorary Doctor of Laws by the University of the West Indies for his achievements in the sport, said he had no regrets and was thankful for all the opportunity that came his way.

The 44 years old made his West Indies debut in 1994 as a teenager and went on to play 164 Tests, 268 ODI's and 22 T20s in an international career that only ended in 2015. He tallied 11,867 Test runs with 30 centuries and 66 half-centuries, for an average of 51,37. In ODIs, the left-hander from Guyana scored 8,778 runs with 11 hundreds and 59 half-centuries.

Speaking after being honoured by UWI in St. Augustine on Thursday, Chanderpaul said he was thankful for everything he has achieved and placed his Honorary Doctor of Laws right up there with his exploits on the field.

"In life. God decides what is for you. So no regrets. I am thankful. I got an opportunity to play and to play for as long as I have done, I have to be very thankful," said Chanderpaul.

"Definitely very excited and thankful to the University also. It is up there. We spend so many years giving to the region and then the University of the West Indies comes and honours you, so I am definitely happy for that and I will count it up there with my other achievements I have done in life. I have done a lot of good things in my career and I have seen some records, Brian's (Lara) record and personally, for me, it is up there," he added.

Looking back at the start of his career, Chanderpaul admitted that he never imagined he would have come this far. "In the first place, when I heard my name I was frozen for a while but then everything started clicking in for me and then I started thinking about the opportunity I was getting," Chanderpaul revealed. "I have seen a lot of good players who never got an opportunity to play so when I realized I got an opportunity, I said I needed to grab this with both hands. I could not let it slide….. and getting to play for the West Indies was a dream come true for me.

"I never really thought my career would have gone that far. In the beginning you are looking to get into the team and try and cement your place, and I was in and out of the team, so I was trying to make myself a permanent member of the team," he continued:

"As you start to get better and cement your place a bit more coming down to the back end of your career, you start thinking about records and what you want to achieve in your career and you are also thinking about your team. You want your team to win. You come from a team in the past that always used to win and you go through all these different eras with different players but you want your team to do well also. The Caribbean people are watching you and they want you to do well also, and sometimes I go out there and I am batting and thinking about all these things and you still have to go out there give a good account of ourselves and hopefully, win a few games and win enough so the people in the Caribbean can be proud of us," Chanderpaul added.

Appendix 2 (Saturday Express 27th October 2018.)

Sports can give youths hope, says Chanderpaul.

"Sports can deter Caribbean youth from a life of crime and violence. And young people can have fun and make exorbitant sums of money from sporting disciplines, including cricket, football and athletics."

Guyana – born Shivnarine "Chanders" Chanderpaul shared this kernel of wisdom on Thursday at The University of West Indies, St Augustine after he was conferred with the degree of Doctor of Law (LLD), Honoris Causa of The UWI. Among those present were Chancellor Robert Bermudez and valedictorian Ayana Dominique Norville, who graduated with a Bachelor of Law, First Class Honours, Faculty of Law.

Later on Chanderpaul, a cricketer extraordinaire, accepted a steady stream of congratulations including from Adult Literacy Tutors Association (Alta) CEO Paula Lucie-Smith who was also conferred with an honorary doctorate for myriad contributions as a teacher, advocate and pioneer.

In an interview with the Express at the University Inn, Chanderpaul said: "I want to thank the university for honouring me for my contribution to sport and public life. I want to advise young people if you do well, university and the country might honour you. I accept the award with a great sense of pride and gratitude on behalf of the people of the region. I want to thank my father, Khemraj Chanderpaul, for his input. It is a tremendous milestone."

Asked how sport can intervene in the lives of Caribbean youth, he said: "Sport can be used to take people away from a life of crime and violence. Sport can give them hope; especially those who come from deprived backgrounds. Sport is a big area. If people play more sports they can have fun and make exorbitant sums of money at the same time. Sports can be lucrative."

Chanderpaul listed Guyanese batsman Alvin Kallicharan, Indian players, Tendulkar and Dravid and Trinidad and Tobago's superstar Brian Lara as his mentors. Chanderpaul's fans have labelled him "Mr Dependable" because of his dexterity, patience and uncanny ability to discern his opponent's next move on the field. Chanderpaul was also named International Cricket Council ICC Cricketer of the year in 2008.

Shivnarine Chanderpaul is a humble legend of West Indies cricket. Born in Guyana, this former West Indies captain is the first cricketer of Indo-Caribbean descent to play over 100 Tests for the West Indies and only the third to have an international career of over two decades. Chanderpaul has scored over 20,000 runs in international cricket and was awarded the International Cricket Council's (ICC) Sir

Garfield Sobers Trophy in 2008. Born and raised in Unity Village, Guyana, his interest in cricket was nurtured by his father from a young age, and by the time he was eight years old he was playing for the village team.

Chanderpaul made his first-class cricket debut for the national team at age 17 and the following year (1993) played for the West Indies Under-19 team in England. He scored an impressive 372 runs during the series, including an outstanding 203 not out in the first Test, making him the team's highest scorer. From there his reputation as a batsman and good all-around cricketer grew.

In his career, Chanderpaul has scored over 11,800 runs in Test cricket, giving him the eight highest total for a Test batsman in history. He has been in several crucial batting partnerships with fellow greats such as Brian Lara and Carl Hooper. In 2004, he became captain of the West Indies team and in the first match in a series against South Africa scored 203 runs not out, making him only the second batsman in history to score a double century in their captaincy debut.

Off the field, Chanderpaul has led many community-level projects in his home village, regional projects in Guyana, and has influenced West Indies policy and practice over the years. His influence as a skilled, focused and hard-working sportsman has extended to many cricket-playing nations. (Courtesy UWI)

Appendix 3

Becoming a Legend – Posted by Stabroek Staff of December 16, 2012 at 5:09am in Features, Sunday.

On Sunday, 19th February 1992 a surprisingly prescient editorial appeared in the Stabroek News. It was not a comment in the sports column. It was the main opinion piece which began as follows:

"Let us be the first West Indian newspaper to editorialise on a young man who one day may make the whole region proud. It is the earliest of days – In fact, his first match for Guyana – and we do not want to swell young Chanderpaul's head, but in the two days he was on show at Bourda he showed a glimpse of the astonishing eye, technique, timing and appetite for runs which one associates with future cricket greatness.

Young Chanderpaul is no more than a boy – the youngest cricketer ever to play for Guyana – and a lot could go wrong. He needs the right training, the right advice, a lot of judicious sport, and naturally, his fair share of luck. He will encounter failure and we will see how he deals with that. However, those who were fortunate enough to see Chanderpaul's batting at Bourda in his first match for his country know that they were in the presence of a very rare talent. There was an aura about the slip of a boy as he batted that was unmistakable."

The frail schoolboy has more than fulfilled those early expectations. He has, quite simply, become one of the very great Guyanese and West Indian batsmen. His slight figure, batting and batting hour after hour, never wavering in determination and concentration and supreme idiosyncratic skill, has become an instantly recognizable symbol of perseverance in the game of cricket. His place in the pantheon of cricketing immortals is absolutely assured.

Chanderpaul could be a dasher with the best of them. There was after his 69 ball century when he smote Australia's attack to all parts of Bourda in 2003 while making the second fastest Test hundred by a West Indian (only the incomparable Viv Richards' 57 ball century against England was faster than his) and in a famous limited over international against Sri Lanka Chanderpaul won the match for West Indies by hitting the last two balls of the game for a four and a mighty six.

But Chanderpaul's great fame is not based on scoring quick runs. Indomitable, he occupies the crease and steadily, inexorably, monumentally the runs accumulate. He has taken out long leases in Test grounds across the world.

Chanderpaul is in a category by himself and deserves the status of a dictionary word, Chanderpaulian, to describe his unique approach and achievement in the art of batting. In a 'So It Go' column not long ago, Dave Martins identified a key factor in Chanderpaul's success as keeping his head still. "Sure," he wrote, "Shiv fidgets and stretches and squirms in advance but when he plays a shot the head is almost completely still, his eyes are fixed on the ball."

That is absolutely correct. Another factor Dave identified was Chanderpaul's compact striking of the ball. It is true.

Despite Chanderpaul's fussiness, the back-lift is completely unfussy, short and compact. Combine these attributes with his deft and precise footwork, his extraordinary ability to leave it to the last moment to play, or not to play, the speeding or the spinning ball and, of course, his iron will-power and blot-everything-else-out concentration and you have the composite portrait of a batsman unique in the annals of the game. He has faced 100 balls on average in every Test innings he has played. Only Dravid (109) and Kallis (105) in the history of Test cricket have been more tenacious, and no other West Indies player comes close – Lara (85). There has been no more gritty batsman. No batsman has more consistently frustrated bowlers.

In an era when West Indies cricket was in precipitous decline Chanderpaul was frequently the stalwart who helped preserve a few bright shreds of pride. And since Brian Lara's retirement he had been the one batsman who in the worst and most distracting of times at least kept us competitive.

Towards the end of Lara's career, Chanderpaul took on more and more of the responsibility of guiding the faltering West Indies batting lineup. Between 2005 and 2008 he scored over 3000 runs at an average of 62.72. And in the 6-year period since Lara's retirement, Chanderpaul's achievements have been world-class. He has scored 15 of his 27 centuries in that hard and perilous period and his average is 70.

No wonder that in a team fallen near to bottom of the Test ladder he has given us reason time and time again to hold our collective West Indians head high. He reached No 1 in the Test batting rankings in 2008-09 and after slipping out of the top ten he astonishingly returned to the top position in April, 2012. For a while, others overtook him – but after his latest exploits in Bangladesh he is again in the No 1 spot. At 38, I wonder if he is the oldest batsman to have achieved the highest standing in the game.

Kamau Brathwaite in his famous poem 'Rites' speaks forcefully about crises in the West Indies team:

When things going good

you cahn touch

we, but let murder start

an, ol man, you cahn fine

a man to hole up de side.

For years and years Shiv Chanderpaul has personified the man "to hold up de side."

So far, Chanderpaul has made 10,696 runs with 27 centuries in 146 Tests with an average of 51.67. The editorial in Stabroek News nearly 21 years ago ended with this hope:

"Let us wish the young man well as he embarks on what we have every reason to hope will be a brilliant career in regional and, in due course, international cricket."

Chanderpaul, at the time still years away from playing for the West Indies, has exceeded such hopes. He has done Guyana and the West Indies exceedingly proud.

Let us now wish for this marvellous veteran a conclusion

which will match the rest of his unique career – and may the conclusion stretch at least a few more wondrous and prolific seasons in the sun.

Career Statistics 1994-2015

Last Career	Test Matches	ODI
Matches	164	268
Runs Scored	11,867	8,778
Batting Average	51.37	41.60
100s/50s	30/66	11/59

vs team	Span (Years)	Match	Inns	No	Runs	HS	Avg	100s	50s
vs Australia	1996-2012	10	38	5	1649	118	49.96	5	11
vs Bangladesh	2002-2014	20	14	8	897	203	149.5	4	3
vs England	1994-2015	36	60	9	2451	147	48.05	5	16
vs India	1994-2013	25	44	10	2171	140	63.85	7	10
vs N Zeland	1995-2014	21	34	7	1232	126	45.62	2	8
vs Pakistan	1997-2011	14	26	3	986	153	42.86	1	6
vs S Africa	1998-2015	23	41	4	1710	203	46.21	5	8
vs S Lanka	2005-2010	7	12	3	378	86	42	0	3
vs Zbabwe	2000-2013	8	11	0	393	108	35.72	1	1

Runs in Calendar Year

Titles	Match	Inns	NO	Runs	HS	Avg	100s	50s
year 1994	5	8	2	303	77	50.5	0	4
year 1995	4	5	2	233	80	77.66	0	3
year 1996	5	9	0	444	82	49.33	0	4
year 1997	10	17	2	627	137	41.8	1	4
year 1998	9	15	1	446	118	31.85	1	2
year 1999	4	8	0	181	70	22.62	0	1
year 2000	8	13	2	448	89	40.72	0	3
year 2001	4	6	0	151	74	25.16	0	1
year 2002	14	22	6	1065	140	66.56	4	6
year 2003	7	14	0	579	109	41.35	3	1
year 2004	10	18	3	715	128	47.66	2	3
year 2005	11	20	3	964	203	56.7	3	3
year 2006	10	18	1	580	97	34.11	0	5
year 2007	4	7	2	558	136	111.6	3	3
year 2008	9	16	7	909	126	101	3	7
year 2009	9	14	1	466	47	35.84	1	3
year 2010	6	9	2	394	166	56.28	1	2
year 2011	8	15	3	646	118	53.83	2	1
year 2012	9	15	5	987	203	98.7	3	5
year 2013	7	12	3	523	122	58.11	2	1
year 2014	7	11	4	497	101	71	1	3
year 2015	4	8	0	151	50	18.87	0	1

Centuries in Test Cricket

No	Score	Against	Pos.	Inn.	Test	Venue
1	137	India	3	1	3/5	Kensington Oval, Bridgetown
2	118	England	4	1	4/6	Bourda, Georgetown
3	140	India	6	1	1/5	Bourda, Georgetown
4	101	India	6	2	3/5	Kensington Oval, Bridgetown
5	136	India	6	2	4/5	Antigua Recreational Grounds, St. John's
6	140	India	5	2	3/3	Eden Gardens, Kol-kata
7	100	Australia	6	1	1/4	Bourda, Georgetown
8	104	Australia	6	4	4/4	Antigua Recreational Grounds, St. John's
9	109	South Africa	7	3	2/4	Kingsmead, Durnan
10	101	Bangla-desh	6	2	2/2	Sabina Park, King-ston
11	128	England	5	2	1/4	Lord's London
12	203	South Africa	5	1	1/4	Bourda, Georgetown
13	127	South Africa	5	2	4/4	Antigua Recreational Grounds, St. John's
14	153	Pakistan	5	3	1/2	Kensington Oval, Bridgetown
15	116	England	5	4	3/4	Old Trafford, Man-chester
16	136	England	5	1	4/4	RiversaideGround, Chester-le-Street

17	104	South Africa	5	1	1/3	St. George's Park, Port Elizabeth
18	118	Australia	5	2	1/3	Sabina Park, Kingston
19	107	Australia	5	2	2/3	Sir Vivan Richards Stadium North sound
20	126	New Zealand	5	1	2/2	Ms Lean Park, Napier
21	147	England	6	2	5/5	Queen's Park Oval POS
22	166	South Africa	4	2	2/3	Warner Park, Basseterre
23	116	India	5	3	3/3	Windsor Park, Roseau
24	118	India	5	1	1/3	Forez Shah Kotla, Delhi
25	103	Australia	5	1	1/3	Kensington Oval, Bridgetown
26	203	Bangladesh	5	1	1/2	Sher-e-Bangla NationalCricket Stadium, Mirpur
27	150	Bangladesh	5	2	2/2	Sheikh Abu Naser Stadium, Khulna
28	108	Zimbabwe	5	2	2/2	Windsor Park, Roseau
29	122	New Zealand	5	1	3/3	Seddon Park, Hamilton Beas
30	101	Bangladesh	5	3	2/2	Beausejour Stadium, Gros Islet

Centuries in One-Day International

No	Score	Against	Pos.	Inn.	S/R	Venue
1	109	India	2	2	81.34	Kensington Oval, Bridgetown
2	150	South Africa	2	1	110.29	Buffalo Park, East London
3	108	New Zealand	2	2	78.26	Beausejour Stadium, Gros Islet
4	101	Pakistan	2	1	71.12	National Stadium, Karachi
5	149	India	2	2	109.55	Vidarbha Cricket Assocaition Ground
6	102	Ieland	2	2	90.26	Sabina Park, King-ston
7	116	England	3	1	95.08	Ebgbaston, Birming-ham
8	127	Zimba-bwe	3	2	92.02	Harare Sports Club
9	107	Pakistan	4	2	71.81	Skeikh Zayed Stadi-um Abu Dhabi
10	112	England	4	1	83.58	Providence Stadium
11	101	Canada	2	1	84.16	Sabina Park, King-ston

Sources of Reference

Arlott, John (ed): Cricket, the Great Captains, Pelham Book 1971

Atherton Mike: Opening Up, Hodder & Stoughton 2002

Beckles, Hilary McD: The Development of West Indies Cricket Vol 1 – The Age of

Blunden,Edmund: Cricket Country

Nationalism, Pluto Press

Beckles, Hilary McD: The Development of West Indies Cricket Vol 2 – The Age of Globalization, Pluto Press 1998

Beckles, Hilary McD ed: The Spirit of Dominance – Cricket and Nationalism in the West Indies, Canoe Press 1998

Beckles, Hilary McD: Cricket Without a Cause, Ian Randle Publishers.

Bose, M: A History of Indian Cricket, Andre Deutsch (Revised) 2002

Brearley M: The Art of Captaincy, Hodder and Stoughton Ltd, 1998

Bright-Holmes J (ed): The Joy of Cricket, Secker and Warburg 1984

Frindall, Bill (ed): The Wisden Book of Test Cricket (2 Vols) Queen Ann Press Book

Goodwin, Clayton: Caribbean Cricketers – from the Pioneers to Packer, Harvey 1980

Grinshaw, Anna (ed): CLR James Cricket, W.H. Allen & Co. 1986

Guha, R: The Picador Book of Cricket, Picador 2001

Guha, R: A Corner of a Foreign Field, Picador 2002

James, CLR: Beyond a Boundary, Hutchinson 1963

James, CLR: Cricket

Keynes, A and Lapidge, M: (translated and introduced by) Alfred The Great, Penguin Books 1983

Lemmom, D: The Guinness Book of Test Cricket Captains, Guinness Publishing

Manley, Michael: The History of the West Indian Cricket, West Indies Publishing 1988

Morris, Mervin and Carnegie, Jimmy: Lunch Time Medley – Writings on Cricket, Ian Randle Publishers.

Narinesingh, Clifford: Gavaskar, Portrait of A Hero, Royards Publishing, 1995

Narinesingh, Clifford: The Presence of Tendulkar, Royards Publishing, 2005
Narinesingh, Clifford: Lara - The Untamed Spirit, RPC, 2009.
Nidamboor, R/Peter Murray: Cricket Boulevard, Murray Books 2004
Perry, Ronald: Bradman's Best, Bantam Press 2001
Ramchand, P: The Captains-Nayadu to Tendulkar, The Marine Sports 1997
Reeve, Dermot: Winning Ways, Boxtree Ltd 1996
Richards, Vivan: Hitting Across the Line, Headline Book Publishing PLC 1991
Roebuck. Peter: Sometimes I forgot to laugh, Allen Unwin, (Australia) 2004
Rosenwater, Irving: Sir Donald Bradman – A Biography
Scovell, Brian: Beating the Field, Partridge Press 1995 with Brian Lara.
Scovell, Brian: Lara, Cricket's Troubled Genius Stadia 2007
Sachin, Tendulkar with Boria Majumdar: Sachin – Playing it My Way, Hodder and Stoughton.
Warne, Shane: My autobiography, Hodder & Stoughton 2001
Waugh, Steve: Out of My comfort Zone, Viking/Penguin Books 2005
Wisden Cricket Monthly /1995-2016
Trinidad guardian
Trinidad Express
Newsday
The Daily Gleaner
The Barbados Advocate
Wikipedia
Cricinfo
Wisden Cricket Almanac 1995-2016

Made in the USA
Coppell, TX
11 November 2022